CHARISMATIC
PRESENCE

Praise for *Charismatic Presence*

"*Charismatic Presence* brings clear, compelling, and candid advice for any professional who wants to speak with more clarity and real impact. Easy to read and hard to put down, this book will change the way the world experiences you as a speaker."

—**Katherine Eitel Belt**, CSP, Founder/CEO of LionSpeak, author of *Something's Gotta Change! Courageous Conversations to Create Clarity and Inspire Change*

"Read this book and refer to it often. It will be your ultimate blueprint in helping you master your craft, and exponentially become a better communicator, presenter, and the leader you were meant to be."

—**Mark LeBlanc**, CSP, CPAE Hall of Fame Speaker, author of *Never Be the Same* and *Growing Your Business!*

"Want to stand out in a sea of boring presentations? Look no further. Eleni shows you how to be present, be yourself, and be memorable! A must-read for anyone who wants to be of lasting influence when speaking to a group or leading a team."

—**Edward Valdez**, Head of Global Training, Sartorius

"There are just a ton of things I love about this book. It's more than the five easy-to-understand principles Eleni Kelakos shares, the stories she tells, or the examples she offers. It's the TONE. Reading it makes you feel like you're sitting on the back porch, shoes off, adult beverage in hand (!) and a really good, really smart friend is sharing her secrets. Get a copy for yourself and a couple more for your pals. You will be so glad. They will, too."

—**Lou Heckler**, Hall of Fame speaker and speaker coach

"A captivating blend of rich prose and expert storytelling, this book offers invaluable insights about the power of presence and becoming a more powerful, confident communicator in any setting."

—**Laura Denton**, Director of Faculty Development, University of Michigan Medical School*

"This book represents years of study and presentation prowess. By applying Eleni Kelakos' Five Principles, you can transform your audience from passive listeners into engaged, enthusiastic fans—captivated, inspired, and drawn to your Charismatic Presence."

—**Naomi Rhode**, CSP, CPAE, Speaker Hall of Fame, Past President National Speakers Association, Past President Global Speakers Federation

CHARISMATIC
PRESENCE

5 Principles For
Magnetic Presentations

ELENI KELAKOS, CSP

INDIE BOOKS
INTERNATIONAL

CHARISMATIC PRESENCE
5 Principles For Magnetic Presentations

To my coaching clients
who have stood, trembling but determined,
in the murky middle of discomfort
in the name of learning and growth.
Keep on using your words to change your world!

And to my brother, George Michael Kelakos,
the Boy Who Ate The World, and the poster child
for Charismatic Presence.

TABLE OF CONTENTS

Preface

I was eleven years old when I was first rewarded with a round of applause meant only for me. I had just finished singing the song *Froggie Went A-Courtin'* all by myself, in a pool of light on a big, wooden outdoor stage in the talent show at summer camp. The audience of parents and campers sitting in lawn chairs on the grass had surprised me by singing along to the chorus and clapping in time to the music. They surprised me again by clapping and hooting wildly.

It was delicious. Heady. Addictive. I loved it and wanted more. And so began my lifelong love of performing.

I was such a natural-born diva, so effortlessly present and comfortable on stage, that I was thrown for a complete loop the first time I got smacked with performance anxiety. It happened in the ninth grade when I was cast as the scheming Queen Aggravain in a production of *Once Upon A Mattress* at the Walworth Barbour American International School in Israel. We had rehearsed for weeks, and I had my lines down cold. At least, I thought I did—until the curtain rose on opening night, and I beheld the whispering, expectant audience.

I remember the butterflies colliding in my stomach, my heart beating so fast I thought it was going to sprout legs and run away from me. Most of all, I remember the complete and utter surprise—not to mention panic—I felt when I couldn't remember my very first line for the life of me. My face hot under the wash of the stage lights, I leaned over to the fellow thespian playing my king and hissed, "What's my line?" Fortunately, my scene partner knew it and whispered it to me. I smiled and spoke the line without missing a beat. The rest of the show went like gangbusters, my lines flowing with ease and confidence. Still, I have never forgotten those moments of uncertainty and vulnerability when, caught like the proverbial deer in the headlights, I was unable to recall lines I thought I could utter in my sleep.

Fortunately, this tender, icky moment didn't scare me off my destined path as a professional actor, singer-songwriter, speaker, and trainer. For many decades now, I've acted, sung, or spoken on countless stages (and screens) both large and small and engaged with audiences as large as thirty-four thousand (Shea Stadium, for a Mets game) and as small as two (the bartender and one drunk patron at a tiny folk club). Through it all, I have learned that performance anxiety can be managed, presentation skills can be improved, and the inherent charisma we all possess can be fanned to a greater, more compelling flame. The countless business professionals I've coached and trained for over two decades have learned this, too, going on to share their messages with greater confidence and impact.

Since I think there's nothing more important than sharing your unique wisdom, ideas, and perspectives with the people who need to hear them, I'm delighted you had the urge to buy this book. You'll be glad you did, as will the members of your audience, who need to hear exactly what you have to say.

Eleni Kelakos
September 2024

PART I

The Stakes Are High

CHAPTER 1

Why Charismatic Presence And Presentation Skills Matter

Presence [is] . . . the real core component of charisma,
the foundation upon which all else is built.
OLIVIA FOX CABANE, THE CHARISMA MYTH[1]

You were born with a powerful, magnetic presence. A presence that's yours to expand and share without a whole lot of muss or fuss. A Charismatic Presence that may very well be different from what you think "presence" and "charisma" looks or feels like.

Don't believe that? I sure didn't. Until the night and the moment when I saw and realized those mind-blowing notions for myself.

It happened in 1988 at a dress rehearsal of an exciting new musical created and performed by a talented cast at the prestigious Humana Festival at the Actors Theatre of Louisville. Slouched in a seat in the darkened theater, I was doing something I often did as a young actor: observing—and learning from—other professional actors as they made their magic on the stage.

3

The cast was large, and the opening musical number was big and bombastic. Actors in colorful costumes danced and sang their hearts out on the brightly lit stage. As they swirled and twirled and sang and whirled, I found my eyes drifting to a small staircase at the very back of the stage. On the stairs sat a little girl, an actor of about eight years old, thoroughly and silently absorbed in reading a large book. I watched her slowly turn page after page of her book, seemingly oblivious to anything going on around her. She wasn't trying to "act." She wasn't trying to make us watch her or like her. She wasn't trying to impress us. She wasn't "trying" at all. She was simply being herself, fully present in the moment, and utterly engaged with her task. And as a result, I couldn't take my eyes off her.

I thought about that little girl long after I left the theater that evening. Because without even trying, she had radiated "it"—that intangible magnetism we call *charisma*.

That little actor had charisma, in the extreme, which both confused and intrigued me. Because, up until that moment, I had equated charisma with a sort of pumped-up, larger-than-life magnetism, and not the compelling, quiet ease and authenticity displayed by an eight-year-old neophyte actor who had been simply reading to herself in public.

What I realized that night was that you can't have charisma without being genuinely present. Thus began my lifelong commitment to learn, embody, and teach the principles that allow for a maximized Charismatic Presence.

So, What Is Charisma And Charismatic Presence? And Who's Got It?

Many people believe, as I once did, that charisma is only embodied and expressed by larger-than-life, super-confident extroverts in a larger-than-life, super-confident manner. They believe that only a chosen few—their verbally dexterous business partner, their charming Aunt Charlotte, their favorite screen idols (Idris Alba! Meryl Streep!)— are blessed with an innate confidence and charisma that lights up a room or stage. They believe that charisma is something you are gifted with, a special intrinsic talent like the ability to sing on pitch or calculate numbers in your head. Most of all, they believe that charisma is something that other people possess and that *you either have charisma or you don't.*

To which I say, *yes and no*. Let me explain.

The *Merriam-Webster.com Dictionary* defines charisma as "a special magnetic charm or appeal."[2] It's derived from the Greek *charestai* ("to favor"), which in turn comes from the noun *charis*, meaning "grace," which, among other things, is defined as a virtue or state of sanctification coming from God. So, I suppose you could argue that some rarified people are "graced" or "gifted" with charisma.

That said, and with all due respect to *Merriam-Webster*, I happen to believe that the essence—the glowing ember—of charisma is in all of us, a part of us from the get-go. We all have what I call Charismatic Presence. If you have ever been transfixed by the sight of a baby simply lying in his crib blowing spit bubbles or a fuzzy kitten happily cleaning herself in a sunbeam, you know what I'm talking about. Little babies, whether they have two legs or four, are utterly magnetic. And just like that little girl on the stage at the Actors Theatre of Louisville, they're not *trying* to be magnetic. They're simply being who they are, fully, in the moment at hand. They're radiating their magnetic, unbridled *life force*—or, as the Greeks say it, their *dynamis* (dynamic or powerful) *zois* (life). (Full disclosure: I'm of Greek background, and, as my Dad used to say, "all the good words come from the Greek").

Taking that a step further, I would define Charismatic Presence as *your dynamic life force fully activated in the present moment.* It's the kind of all-senses-go, ease, aliveness, and authenticity that makes people want to look at you, listen to you, and trust you. Even if all you're doing is quietly reading a book on a crowded stage.

Your Charismatic Presence is like the pilot light on a gas stove, always in the "on" position. It can smolder at a low glow, or burst into a mesmerizing, warming flame, depending on your willingness to feed it and tend it. The brighter the flame of your Charismatic Presence, the greater your ability to affect and influence your audience of one or many.

The expression of Charismatic Presence is as varied, nuanced, and unique as there are people on this planet. Put another way, your Charismatic Presence is imbued with the flavor and feel of your unique personality. Its rich warmth is what allows you to connect to audiences large and small, build the relationships that build your business, and effectively lead your teams to success. If you want to be a masterful public speaker, cultivating a maximized Charismatic Presence that is consistent under pressure and scrutiny is downright essential. And the responsibility for feeding, tending, and boosting the flame of your Charismatic Presence is yours alone.

You Can Boost Your Charismatic Presence

Charismatic Presence is something the clients I coach and train long to have (not realizing they have it already). What they want—to be fully themselves when others are watching them; to give a public presentation without being broadsided by nerves; to confidently own the stage, boardroom, or meeting while moving others into feeling and action—seems, to them, to be utterly, depressingly, out of reach.

But I know it isn't.

As a New York and Hollywood actor and singer-songwriter who learned how to be more consistently and charismatically present in spotlight moments, and a presentation skills expert who works with executives who want to connect more effectively with an audience and have more impact and influence, here's what I know: You don't need to somehow cultivate "magical" qualities outside yourself like charm, star power, pizzazz, or allure to be a powerful public speaker. You need to allow yourself to get out of your way so you can reconnect with and uncover your naturally magnetic Charismatic Presence.

I know that with the right tools and methodologies, you can overcome the factors that dampen Charismatic Presence—such as worrying too much about making a mistake or what your audience is thinking or being overwhelmed by performance anxiety. And I know inherent Charismatic Presence can be maximized, just as I know that ho-hum speakers can become good speakers and good speakers can become great speakers—if they choose to and if they get the guidance they need.

I'm in full agreement with author Olivia Fox Cabane, who writes in her book, *The Charisma Myth*, that "Charisma is not magic; it's learned behaviors." Presence ". . . turns out to be the real core component of charisma, the foundation upon which all else is built."[3]

In a sense, it's all about learning (or relearning) how to be Present with a capital *P* and daring to be fully who you are when others are watching—especially in a high-stress, high-stakes public-speaking spotlight moment.

Like Peas And Carrots, Charisma And Public Speaking Go Together

In my mind (and work), Charismatic Presence and public speaking prowess go hand in hand. When I'm coaching a client on the latter, I'm typically working with them on the former. Each informs the other.

For those in leadership positions, being able to "own the room"—meaning allowing one's Charismatic Presence to fill the space and touch hearts and souls—is essential if they want to be of real influence. So is being able to communicate, pitch, and present clearly, cogently, and persuasively to an audience of one or many. As I like to say, "Great leaders are great speakers. And great speakers are great leaders."

Presentation skills matter. In fact, billionaire Warren Buffett, arguably one of our time's most influential thought leaders and business executives, has often been quoted as saying that public speaking abilities are the single most important business skills you can have. And this is from a man who initially dropped out of a Dale Carnegie public speaking class because he was, ironically, afraid he'd be asked to get up and speak. Buffett eventually sucked it up and went back to class. He considers the diploma he received when he graduated from that Dale Carnegie course, which he proudly displays in his office, one of his most important achievements. That's why, when he was delivering an address to a graduating class at Columbia Business School, he said, ". . . you can improve your value by fifty percent just by learning communication skills—public speaking."[4]

Buffett understood the importance of being able to share an idea in a way that moves people into feeling and action. To do that, not only do you need to have a good grasp of the nuts and bolts of public speaking, but you've got to be able to maximize your Charismatic Presence in spotlight moments that can feel downright scary.

Nothing dials down your Charismatic Presence more than the *F* word.

No, not that *F* word.

I'm talking about *fear*.

Fear: The Real F Word

"I want you to give a presentation."

How do you feel when you read those words?

Do they make you beam with joy and quiver with anticipation? If so, you're one of the lucky 10 percent of people polled who leap at the chance to speak in public.[5] I call you the "Yay-ers."

Do the words make you sphincter up, cringe, and want to run like hell for the hills? Then you're one of the 10 percent of the population for whom public speaking is a dreaded, hateful task that is best avoided at all costs. I call you the "Nay-ers."

Does the statement make you shrug and say "whatever"? Then you're part of the remaining 80 percent of the population that hovers, uncertain, in the murky middle between love and hate of public speaking. I call you "Ehh-ers." When Ehh-ers give a presentation, they do it grudgingly. They do it because they've got to. They do it because if they don't, they'll lose their job, their standing, the sale, their self-respect. They do it because, as stressful as the experience might be, they know it will eventually be over, and they will have, somehow, survived. Furthermore, when Ehh-ers give a public presentation, it often lacks consistency, confidence, color, and clarity, reflecting both their underlying anxiety and their "I-can-take-it-or-leave-it" level of commitment.

For the Ehh-ers (and the small number of Nay-ers who get roped into speaking in public despite their efforts to avoid it) fear plays a major factor in their attitude and experience: fear of looking bad, saying the wrong thing, forgetting their words; fear of flushing, trembling, or sweating publicly; fear of being laughed at, dismissed, and not good enough. And because of those fears, they shut down, shut up, and hide, defaulting to a vanilla version of who they really are. As a result, the world loses out on the gifts, the wisdom, the insights, and the expertise that they alone can provide.

When we're little babies, or in the early years of our existence, like that girl on the stage at the Actor's Theatre of Louisville, we haven't yet been battered into submission by a plethora of "no" and "don't be you" served up to us by the greater world. However, once we step into the greater world and start to care (often too much) about what other people think of us, or being perfect at all costs, or impressing (or disappointing) others, we capitulate to fear and risk, becoming self-conscious and self-limiting. We pull back and play small, diminishing the Charismatic Presence that is our birthright. This is why every time I'm in a restaurant and witness a parent tell their exuberant, loudly chatting child, "Shh. Honey. Use your indoor voice," I think, "And so it begins."

When it comes down to it, fear can keep your Charismatic Presence burning too low to make the kind of difference that turns heads, moves hearts, and cements deals.

That's what fear can do.

I know all about this kind of fear because I had to learn to overcome it myself as a young actor to manage auditions, interviews, and performances. The tools I learned under the tutelage of master-level acting teachers in New York City are the very same tools I've been sharing with my clients since I hung up my shingle as a presence and presentation coach and trainer oh lo these many years. Day in and day out, I happily help fretting Nay-ers, Ehh-ers (and Yay-ers, too) overcome their performance anxiety; organize, practice, and deliver effective presentations; and maximize their Charismatic Presence. Because I know, and they know, that—whether it's presenting a quarterly report at a board meeting, delivering a keynote at a major conference, or toasting a family member on their wedding day—opportunities and obligations to speak in public are a fact of life, and a given in the business world. And if they don't come through to the best of their abilities in critical spotlight moments, their work, career, and reputation can suffer.

Sky-High Stakes

When it comes to expressing why they need to learn to speak to groups with less fear, more confidence, and greater Charismatic Presence, my clients—CEOs, middle managers, financial services experts, IT professionals, engineers, salespeople, and business owners—are dead clear about what's at stake:

"If I don't learn to manage my fear of public speaking, I'll never sell my services."

"If I can't convey my big idea fearlessly and effectively, it won't get funded."

"If I keep avoiding giving presentations, I'm never going to get promoted."

"If I can't inspire my team to embrace my vision, we're going to keep underperforming and losing money."

The fact is, the inability to speak effectively in public can cost you customers, keep you from motivating your team, and damage your career prospects.

And yet, even in the face of these facts, people still find ways to back out of critical public speaking engagements (hello again, Nay-ers). In an article he wrote for *Forbes*, Carmine Gallo pointed to the findings of a survey that underscored the remarkable measures people will take to avoid giving presentations. Apparently, 20 percent of respondents would do practically anything to avoid giving a presentation, including pretending to be sick.[6]

I've seen my share of presentation avoidance with many of my own clients. Over the years, I've coached smart, accomplished business professionals who admitted they changed their majors in college because they were terrified of having to take a required public speaking course. I've worked with people who lied about being sick or having been in a car accident rather than get up and give a business presentation. I've coached people who have admitted to turning down promotions or threatening to quit their jobs to avoid giving public presentations. And I've worked with numerous executives who have regularly (and sheepishly) handed off public speaking opportunities to other colleagues, even though they knew their unwillingness to take the stage hurt their career or reputation.

Ironically, the more you let the fear of public speaking stop you from speaking in public, the less confident you feel about public speaking, and the less you want to speak in public. The less you speak in public, the less confident you feel about speaking in public, and the more your Charismatic Presence takes a hit. It's a vicious circle.

That said, you don't have to let fear of public speaking or feelings of inadequacy or discomfort around your public speaking abilities stop you. If you choose, you can learn to overcome performance anxiety and improve your ability to create and deliver a solid and persuasive presentation.

As with any other skill set—like tennis, cooking, or driving—better public speaking skills and the confidence (and Charismatic Presence) that goes with them can be acquired with time and practice.

The Rich Rewards Of Presentation Skills Mastery

What do you stand to gain by putting in the kind of time, effort, and focus that moves you from fear to fearlessness and from "ehh" to "yay" as a presenter? Well, to borrow a line from the poet Elizabeth Barrett Browning's *Sonnet 43*, ". . . let me count the ways."[7]

For one thing, your confidence will take a great leap forward. And the more confident you feel, the more presence you exude, and the more attractive and magnetic you become.

Another result of improving your presentation skills is a better ability to lead a team. This means more productivity and a better bottom line.

Then, there's the ability to attract more business and customers. I have said time and again that there's no better way to attract customers than to give a public presentation that not only teaches them something of value but helps them feel what it might be like to work with you. I have built my business through these kinds of "showcases" and encourage my clients to do the same.

And let's not discount a huge advantage to acquiring better presentation skills: increasing the perception of you as a thought leader and expanding your visibility and reach.

Improving your presentation skills will also help you stand out above the majority of employees (or prospective employees) whose soft skills are sadly lacking. In fact, according to an article in *Education Week* by Catherine Gewertz, survey data reveals that the one soft skill employers struggle to find in new hires and want more than anything (even before critical thinking, working with teams, and writing well) is good speaking skills. Intangible "soft" skills, like presentation skills, can have a great deal of impact on your ability to get a job, motivate a team to complete a project, and persuade an investor to fling money at your big idea.[8]

As author and member of the National Speakers Association CPAE Speaker Hall of Fame Mark Le Blanc, CSP, likes to say, "Intangibles drive the tangibles."

Perhaps the biggest argument in favor of gaining presentation skills mastery is being able to say "yes" to speaking at the pivotal personal-but-public occasions that life serves up—like giving the eulogy at your dad's funeral, delivering the best man's speech at your buddy's wedding reception, or saying a few gracious words of thanks for a well-deserved award at a business event. These are moments of grace you might miss (and later regret) if you choose to turn them down due to fear or discomfort at the thought of standing in the spotlight and speaking to a group.

Now Is The Time

The fact that you bought this book and are reading it right now tells me that the time is right for you to do what it takes to maximize your Charismatic Presence and your presentation skills. The sooner you plunge in and do the work, the sooner you'll find relief from the fear or lack of confidence that plagues you—and the sooner you can make a greater difference at work and in the world.

Whether you want to be able to deliver your company's quarterly numbers report with more punch and personality, or give a guest sermon at your local church, what you have to say matters. And if you're willing to go the distance with me through the chapters of this book and embrace the five presence principles, you'll shift your attitude about public speaking, maximize your Charismatic Presence, and shine on the speaking platform.

CHAPTER 2

Oh! Say Can You See What An Actor Can Teach You About Presence And Presentation Skills

Come on to the theater!
Hi-diddle-dee-dee
An actor's life for me
A high silk hat and a silver cane
A watch of gold with a diamond chain
Lyrics from the Walt Disney Studios film *Pinocchio*[9]

You may be wondering: What exactly are the five principles of Charismatic Presence, anyway? Well, as a little tease, here they are in a nutshell:

- **Know thyself.** Do what it takes to identify your *blessings* (talents, abilities, and gifts) and *blocks* (the limiting beliefs that lead to limiting behaviors).

- **Be thyself.** Be willing to show up fully, revealing yourself as you genuinely are, in all your beautiful, magnetic vulnerability.

15

- **Prepare thyself.** Honor the stage and the moment by being ready. This includes prepping and practicing the material that serves as a vehicle for your ideas and wisdom as well as maximizing your three presence planes (physical, vocal and energetic).

- **Commit thyself.** Stay focused on staying in the moment and honoring your intention (what you're there to *do*), even if it's challenging.

- **Turn thyself on.** Wake up the three presence planes that make up your Charismatic Presence by embracing and using your unique gifts and talents. Because when you're engaged and energized, your audience is too.

The Five Principles: Simple, But Not Easy

It's taken me years to clarify, conceptualize, and understand these five principles.

It's also taken me years to embody them. And even as I write this, I think *I'm not done yet*. Because the five principles come together to create presence and presentation mastery. And mastery in any field, whether it's acting, golfing, public speaking, or boat building, is a lifetime endeavor requiring lifelong learning.

That said, "mastery" is not an end unto itself. Developing mastery in exuding a consistent Charismatic Presence is a process, not a static result—a process that takes time, patience, and commitment. It is a process that is guided by the lessons learned and gifts unveiled in the exploration of the five presence principles.

Top-level actors are devoted to the process of developing themselves over a lifetime. They clearly understand the concept of fueling their ability to live fully in the moment, all systems go, in front of an audience. I call this "moving toward mastery."

To do this, they continuously take classes (scene study, voice lessons, dance) that push them to overcome limitations and gain greater confidence and competence. They are constantly developing their physical and vocal abilities. They also gravitate toward projects that excite them (thus fanning the flame) and frighten them (due to the inherent challenges that the roles present).

For example, Peter Dinklage, best known for his acclaimed appearance as Tyrion Lannister in the television series *Game of Thrones*, isn't exactly much of a singer or sword fighter. Yet those were the very skills he needed to learn when he decided to take on the swashbuckling role of Cyrano de Bergerac, a heroic soldier, in the 2021 movie musical *Cyrano*. Why did he do it? Because he was attracted by the challenge of going beyond his comfort zone. "I've got to be intimidated by it," he explained. "Anything that scares me gets my interest."[10]

Multiple Emmy Award-winning actor Julia Louis-Dreyfus, who is known for her comedic skills as the star of such TV shows as *Veep* and *Seinfeld*, recently chose to embark on an era of doing what scares her. This includes taking on darker, more dramatic roles, like a mother facing the impending death of her sick child in the film *Tuesday*. "Challenge yourself," she is quoted as saying, "and do things that give you a little bit of a butterfly feeling. That's why I did [*Tuesday*]."[11]

Moving toward mastery by continuously leaning in toward what challenges them is what makes great actors (and speakers, and athletes), great. It also ratchets up confidence, consistency, and charisma.

Actors Can Teach You A Lot About Maximizing Charismatic Presence

The fact is, there's a lot to learn from actors about managing the fear that can stop you so you can maximize your Charismatic Presence, especially if you want to give speeches and presentations that light up the stage and galvanize your audience.

Now, you may be thinking: "Wait a minute—isn't acting fake? Isn't it basically pretending to be something you're not?"

No, and again, no. At its core, acting is truth-telling. Great actors learn to uncover their truth, sharing what they know to realize the material at hand. And they do it with a full commitment to being present in the moment, right here and right now.

This is exactly what you must do if you want to be the kind of presenter and public speaker who moves your audience into feeling and action. You must be willing to reveal your perspective, your truth, and your yumminess (yes, that is a professional word) if you want to realize the material and be of the greatest service to your audience. Standing in—and radiating—your truth is at the core of your Charismatic Presence. And it's what makes spoken presentations come alive.

As a young actor in New York City, I fiercely embraced this attitude of "learn and improve, lean into what scares you." It's why I signed up for challenging dance classes that made me sweat and struggle, coached with an exacting voice teacher to increase my vocal range and power, and began to fish around for a professional acting class that could push me toward greater levels of excellence.

It was right around this time I was invited to be the guest singer at the Dutch Treat Club in Manhattan, a private monthly luncheon established in 1933 that gathers some of America's greatest creative minds. The guest speaker that day was the then-manager of the New York Mets baseball team, Frank Cashen. When I was through singing, Mr. Cashen stepped up to the podium and declared, "Eleni needs to sing the 'Star-Spangled Banner' at a Mets game." I immediately corralled him and asked for his business card. That afternoon, I called the Mets business office and set the wheels in motion for a day and a moment that would change me forever.

My Shea Stadium Debacle

I'm twenty-four years old, living in New York City, and just starting out as a professional singer and actor when I'm invited to give the most important performance of my young life: singing the national anthem at a Mets game at Shea Stadium in front of thirty-four thousand people.

That's a lot of eyeballs.

Am I nervous? You betcha. Am I excited? Heck, yeah!

Wearing my best dress, I stand waiting in a gated holding area within pinching distance of the players. I am agog, giggly, and gleeful: "Holy cow. This is a dream come true."

I peruse the playing field, noting the microphone that has been positioned between the pitcher's mound and home plate and the gigantic Jumbotron TV screen on which my face and performance will be broadcast to the stadium.

A tap-tap-tap on my shoulder whirls me around. I come face-to-face with a grizzled old groundskeeper, peering up at me.

"Did you know," he says, in a thick Jersey accent, "that the great Broadway singer, Robert Goulet, forgot the words to the national anthem?" Then, he unlatches the gate and ushers me onto the field.

And as I walk toward the waiting microphone, all I can think of is, "Robert Goulet forgot the words. He forgot the words. And if Robert Goulet forgot the words, I could forget the words."

I position myself in front of the microphone, my heart pounding in my ears. I open my mouth and start to sing:

"Oh say, can you see . . .."

It takes at least two endless seconds for the words I sing to blast back at me through the massive stadium speakers. No one warned me about the audio delay. It's so distracting. OMG—Robert Goulet forgot the words!

Rattled, I soldier on:

"What so proudly we hailed, at the twilight's lasts gleaming . . ."

Robert Goulet forgot the words—Robert Goulet.

And then it happens:

"Whose bright stripes and broad . . . uhm . . . stars?"

Bright stripes and broad stars? That is so wrong.

And just like that, I've gone and done it. Just like Robert Goulet, I've messed up the words to the national anthem in front of a stadium full of people who are singing along and know the words.

Somehow, I muddle through the rest of the song. When I'm done, I stumble off the field with tears in my eyes. Because thirty-four thousand Mets fans, not to mention all my relatives watching on TVs up and down the Eastern Seaboard, have not seen me perform at my peak.

Looking back, I realize that was the day I understood just how powerful fear could be.

Because I was afraid of messing up, I messed up.

It's as simple as that.

Yes, I had a little help from my pal, the groundskeeper, whose unfortunate words planted the seed of doubt in my mind. But I watered and nurtured that seed with every step I took toward that microphone. My Charismatic Presence got smaller and smaller with every limiting thought I entertained.

After the fateful experience I now call "my Shea Stadium debacle," I couldn't shake the fear that I would mess up again in a public performance. This fear snaked its way through the auditions and interviews that were an essential part of my obtaining work as a performer, dinging my confidence and dimming my presence. Despite a goodly amount of natural talent and enthusiasm, my level of confidence—and therefore presence—when I performed under pressure went up and down like a yo-yo, depending on who was watching and how high the stakes.

When a casting director who typically championed my work told my agent after an audition, "Eleni just didn't bring her sizzle this time around," I knew I was in trouble. I knew that if I wanted to book acting jobs—and, more importantly, honor my talents and feel satisfied with my auditions—I needed to learn how to consistently perform at my peak while being highly scrutinized. I needed, in effect, to develop a consistent presence under pressure.

So, I did what any actor worth their salt does when they get stuck and stalled in their march toward performance mastery: I went to master-level acting teachers who ultimately taught me techniques and methodologies that allowed me to manage limiting beliefs and behaviors and build on my natural assets. In the end, this allowed me to bring a consistently confident, relaxed, and authentic presence to my performances.

This is why, when I got a call a year after my so-called "Shea Stadium debacle" from the Mets corporate office asking me if I wanted to sing the national anthem again, I said "yes." I knew I was ready to return to the scene of the crime and practice what I'd learned.

This time, I avoided the groundskeeper like the plague.

This time, I stepped in front of the microphone, opened my mouth, and knocked the song right out of the park, every word perfect. And if that wasn't awesome enough, the friend who went to the game with me caught a fly ball, and the Mets won.

The tools and techniques I learned on the dusty stages of acting classes through the masterful tutelage of Michael Howard, James O. Barnhill, and Warren Robertson helped me claim the stage at Shea Stadium that day and on countless days since. They are the methodologies that form the foundation of the five presence principles, and cornerstones of my coaching and training practice. The five presence principles have helped countless executives show up, step up, and speak up with courage, confidence, and authenticity when giving speeches, pitches, and presentations.

I'm betting they'll help you do that, too.

PART II

The Charismatic Presence Process

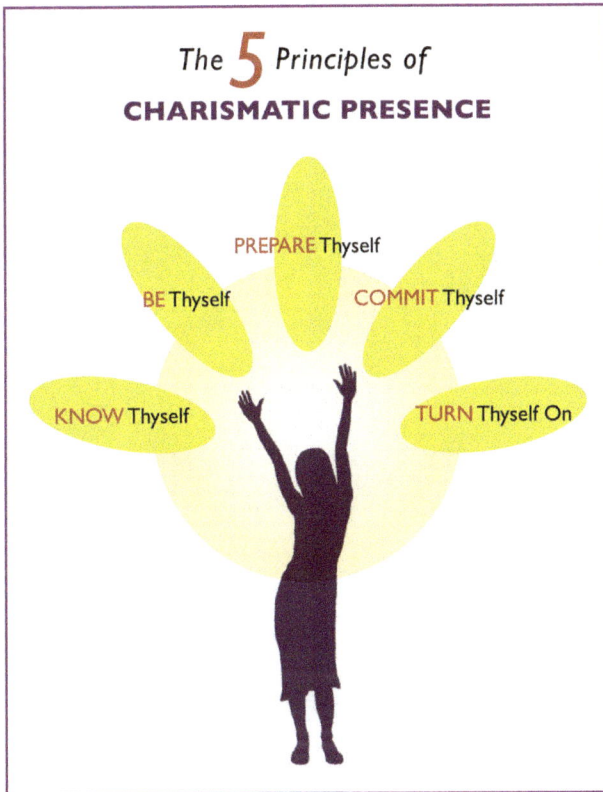

The **5** Principles of
CHARISMATIC PRESENCE

PREPARE Thyself

BE Thyself

COMMIT Thyself

KNOW Thyself

TURN Thyself On

CHAPTER 3

Presence Principle One:
Know Thyself

Knowing yourself is the beginning of all wisdom.
ARISTOTLE, ANCIENT GREEK PHILOSOPHER AND SCIENTIST

"Derek," a soft-spoken man in his forties, had only been CEO of his large corporation for two months when we sat down together for an initial coaching session.[12]

As Derek put it, he was "sweating bullets" at the prospect of giving his first prepared talk to several thousand employees at a company-wide event one month away.

"I'm an introvert," he confessed, "and the idea of all those eyes judging me terrifies me. I've never been much good at public speaking, but it's expected of me in this position. I've got to be able to come through."

"Tell me a little more about yourself as a speaker," I prodded. "What do you do well, and what do you struggle with?"

"Well," he said, leaning back in his leather chair, "I'm at my best when I can be more spontaneous and work off of bullet points instead of reading from a script. I've never been good at reading aloud, even when

I was a kid in school. If I've got to give a formal, written speech, I obsess about getting it perfect. So, if I stumble over a word, I start talking fast and hyperventilating. Plus, I like small meetings where I can really talk to people. So, the bigger the group, the less I can connect with them, and the more anxious I feel."

"Derek," I said, "you already have a strong grasp of what you're good at and what you're not so good at, which is where our work begins. In the next couple of sessions, let's get even more clear about your strengths and limitations as a speaker, including any limiting beliefs you might have. Then, we can create a presentation and an approach to learning and delivering it that takes advantage of what you do well and minimizes what's getting in the way."

Derek's willingness to see himself and his abilities as they really were in that space and time is a key element of the first principle of the Charismatic Presence process: *Know thyself.*

Know Thyself: The First Presence Principle

As a woman of Greek heritage, it seems fitting that the words of my first presence principle, "know thyself," can be found carved into the ancient stones of the entrance to the temple of the god Apollo in Delphi, Greece.[13] *That's how important they are.*

Know thyself is the first and most essential of my five presence principles. To achieve presence and presentation mastery, you must be willing to think like an actor and devote yourself to the process of getting to know thyself, particularly as it relates to your speaking abilities and ability to be relaxed and present with eyes on you.

Actors utterly embrace the first presence principle—so much so that they typically get a bad rap for their tendency to focus on themselves. The fact is great actors (like great speakers) spend their lifetimes learning all about who they are and what they're made of (the good, the bad, and the ugly) so they can bring greater authenticity and authority to their work.

Great actors (and speakers) understand that they are only as good as their awareness and mastery of their strengths and their liabilities—or what I call their "blessings" and their "blocks." That's why actors worth their salt challenge themselves to explore every aspect of themselves: what they think and believe; what they're good, or not so good, at (e.g., comedy versus drama, scripted versus improvised); what turns them on or off emotionally and energetically.

As a young actor, I was unflinching in my willingness to identify my blessings and my blocks. That awareness came in handy the day I went to meet a prestigious Hollywood film and TV agent in hopes she'd be interested in representing me.

When I stepped into her office, she didn't even bother with "Hello."

"Oh my God," she cried, jumping up from her chair, "you are physically perfect for a role in a new series that's casting right now. Are you funny?"

I stopped in my tracks. "Nice to meet you, too," I thought.

"Yes," I shot back, "I'm funny. I'm great with comedy."

"What about drama? This series is a dramedy. Can you do drama?" The agent snatched my picture and resume out of my hand and quickly perused my credits.

"Yep," I said, "I'm as comfortable with drama as I am with comedy."

"Can you do an Italian accent?" she asked, eyeing me like an eagle.

"Uh-huh. I speak some Italian, and I can do an Italian accent. In fact, I've played an Italian woman in an off-Broadway show and in a commercial."

"What about improv? The director likes to have his actors improvise in auditions and on the set."

"I've had lots of experience with improv and am really good coming up with dialogue and ideas in the moment," I replied.

"Great!" the agent exclaimed, reaching for her phone. "Now, sit down in that chair while I get you an audition for the series."

She wasn't kidding. Two hours later, I was off to my first Hollywood audition. And all because I had been dead sure of what I was good at.

Had the agent asked, I would also have been perfectly candid about sharing what I knew to be my limitations as a performer. For example, if she had asked me about my dancing abilities, I might have said, "I've taken a ton of dance classes, and I'm a 'mover-weller.' This means that I dance well enough to play a leading role but not well enough to be in the chorus line. And honestly, you really don't want to see me try to tap-dance."

I tell this story to make the point that speakers, like actors, need to know and explore the boundaries of their blessings and their blocks. Put another way, they need to have clarity and awareness around how they are coming across in their three presence planes.

The Three Presence Planes: The Bedrock Of Charismatic Presence

When I'm evaluating a client's Charismatic Presence, I look at, listen to, and feel what they are projecting through the three presence planes: verbal, physical, and energetic.

Verbal presence is what you project through the way you use your words and voice.

Physical presence is what you convey by how you sit, stand, walk, and otherwise fill the space around you in your "meat suit" (the body you've been blessed with).

Energetic presence is the feeling or vibe you exude, which either draws people to you or pushes them away; your energetic presence is often determined by your beliefs.

The 3 PLANES of
CHARISMATIC PRESENCE

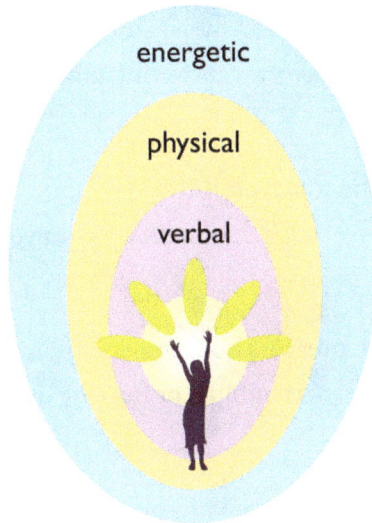

energetic

physical

verbal

As a speaker, the more willing you are to think like an actor and examine your blessings and your blocks in relationship to your three presence planes, the more effective you can be as a communicator.

That's why, if you were sitting down with me as a coaching client like Derek, whose story opened this chapter, I'd spend our first session peppering you with very specific questions that would help me uncover and understand your blessings and blocks. Once we determine where you're stuck or stopped and what's keeping you there, we'd pinpoint and practice the techniques you need to help you think and behave differently, encouraging a greater, more authentic, and effective Charismatic Presence in your speeches, presentations, and communications.

I call the initial phase of the know thyself process *excavation work* or *doing a little digging*. It's like planting a garden: You always start by getting the soil ready for planting, so that the seeds you plant can grow to their fullest potential. This requires digging down and getting your hands dirty.

To Know Thyself, Do A Little Digging

Doing a little digging (or self-analysis) so that you can achieve presence and presentation mastery involves answering numerous thought-provoking questions, such as:

- On a scale of one to ten, if one were "none" and ten were "panic-attack time," how much fear or anxiety do you typically feel when you give a presentation?

- How does your presentation anxiety typically affect your three presence planes (e.g., trembling or freezing up, mind shutting down, talking too fast)?

- Have you ever had a traumatic presentation experience? How do you think it has affected you going forward?

- What is the best presentation experience you've ever had? Why?

- What do you think you do well as a presenter?

- What challenges are you experiencing when you speak or present?

- In what kind of circumstances (audience, setting) are you at your best as a speaker? At your worst?

These are just a few of the relevant and useful questions I might ask a coaching client. That said, the most important question of all is this:

What are the fear-based beliefs that hold you back as a speaker?

The answers to this question, in particular, pave the way for the deepest of "aha!" moments. Because they force you to come face-to-face with your inner naysayers, Moe and Schmoe, whose job it is to trip you up and make you play small in high-stakes spotlight moments.

Meet Moe And Schmoe, Your Nasty Little Naysayers

I imagine Moe and Schmoe as two invisible little gremlins sitting on your shoulder, hissing negative, fear-based beliefs (or what I call lies that bind) into your ears.

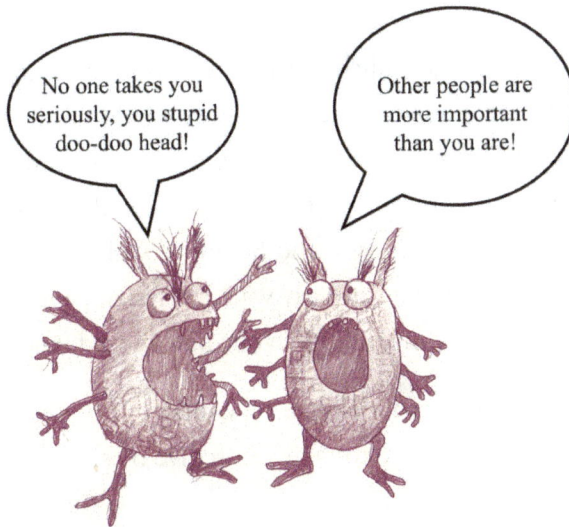

Reframe the Lies That Bind

No one takes you seriously, you stupid doo-doo head!

Other people are more important than you are!

Here's how I described Moe and Schmoe in my book *Claim the Stage: A Woman's Guide to Speaking Up, Standing Out, and Taking Leadership:*

"As the keepers of your deepest fears and limiting beliefs, Moe and Schmoe's job is to make you second-guess yourself when eyes are on you and the stakes are high. They are like little henchmen hired by the brain's amygdala big boss to scare you into taking, or not taking, action based on a perceived threat or fear ('If you don't pay by Thursday, we're gonna come back and break your legs.')"[14]

The amygdala is a part of the brain sometimes referred to as the emotional or irrational brain. It's the part of your brain that takes over—literally hijacking your rational brain—and pushes you into a fight, flight, or freeze response when you're confronted by something potentially life-threatening, such as a fire, or a predator stalking you on a dark night.

If the amygdala could talk, it would probably sound a little like Tony Soprano, the Mafia boss from the HBO TV series *The Sopranos* played by James Gandolfini—tough and gruff with a Jersey accent—and it would say something like this:

"Look, lady, I'm basically here to protect you from stuff that could hurt you. Without me, your caveman ancestors would have probably walked straight up to a saber-toothed tiger and gotten eaten, and you and the rest of the human race wouldn't be here today. All I'm doing is looking out for you, okay? And my boys, Moe and Schmoe? Well, I know they can be a little harsh, but they're like an early warning system, a little reminder that if you're not careful, you could get your butt kicked. Capisce?"

Moe and Schmoe can kick you off course in a presentation and cause your Charismatic Presence to take a nosedive by slamming you with lies that bind like these:

Nobody's going to take what you say seriously.

Everybody can tell you're nervous.

You're going to forget what you wanted to say and look foolish in front of everyone.

You're not qualified to speak about this subject.

And the list goes on.

"I'm Not A Good Speaker": Miho's Story

It's remarkable how many brilliant, capable people allow themselves to be brow-beaten and defeated by Moe and Schmoe and the lies that bind. This was the case for Miho, the extremely warm, funny, and capable owner of a healthcare company, who had this to say—again and again—at our first coaching session:

"I'm not a good speaker."

"Hmm," I thought, "that's a big ol' lie that binds."

The next time she repeated those words, I stopped her in her tracks.

"Miho," I said, "the words you keep repeating, 'I'm not a good speaker,' reflect a limiting lie that binds. What you think and say determines how you behave and perform. So, we're going to work on expunging that lie that binds from your brain and replacing it with a more useful belief. And starting right now, I'd like you to commit to never again saying the words 'I'm not a good speaker' during our meetings. I promise I will stop you in mid-sentence if you do."

I was good to my word, calling out Miho on her limiting belief every time she spoke it aloud. Soon, she was catching herself in mid-statement with a giggle and a rueful eye roll. Over time, and with conscious work, she replaced her limiting belief with one that was more useful. The less she capitulated to her limiting belief, the more her confidence grew as a speaker.

I was so proud of Miho because I understood how challenging it can be to dislodge a lie that binds. That's because positive or negative beliefs, which drive behavior, reside in our subconscious minds—and our subconscious minds are incredibly powerful. In fact, according to Dr. Bruce Lipton, a brain specialist and author of *The Biology of Belief,* subconscious programming in our minds are in control 95 percent of the time. They're essentially steering the ship. That's why it takes sixty-six days to change a physical habit (like chewing your fingernails)[15] and sixty-three days to shift a limiting belief (like "I'm too shy to give public presentations") to one that's more empowering.[16]

I like to compare limiting beliefs to centipedes, which are long, wriggly arthropods that have between just over a dozen and many dozens of legs. Those legs carry poison. If one lands on you, and you scare it, it will thrust its little legs into your flesh, and if you try to rip it off your skin, it will leave its legs—and its venom—behind.

Negative thoughts are like those centipede legs, firmly embedding themselves into your subconscious mind, and difficult to rip away. Making things worse is the fact that your brain remembers negative experiences (like giving a presentation and drawing a blank in front of your boss) more vividly and for a longer time than positive experiences.

That's why it's so important to explore and then expunge old, limiting beliefs that hold you back—to pick out and discard those little centipede legs one by one.

As Miho discovered, expunging a lie that binds takes consciousness, commitment, and hard work.

Managing The Lies That Bind: Four Steps

When I'm working to help a client shift a limiting belief that is affecting their ability to perform at their peak, I take them through a four-step process:

1. **Pinpoint the lies that bind.** Capture your lies that bind on paper as if Moe and Schmoe are speaking them to you. For example, I had Miho make a comprehensive list of her lies that bind that included "You're not a good speaker" and "Everyone can tell you're nervous."

2. **Rate your lies that bind.** Once Miho had listed her lies that bind, I had her rate each one individually on a scale of fear or anxiety

from one to five (one equaled "almost none" and five equaled "off the charts."). That allowed us to determine which of her lies that bind were most "hot button" (typically the fours and fives).

3. **Turn the lies that bind into power phrases.** Rephrasing your lies that bind into more useful and empowering phrases is critical to the process of shifting your beliefs. The idea is to go to the core of the issue represented by the power phrase and turn it inside out like a sock. Keep it positive and in the present moment as if it's already a done deal (no "I will" or "someday"). For example, Miho shifted from "I'm not a good speaker" to "With each session I have with Eleni, and each presentation I give, I am growing better and more confident as a speaker." If you struggle with rephrasing a lie that binds that is especially anxiety provoking, try starting the power phrase with "I am willing to believe that . . ."

4. **Internalize the power phrases.** Repetition, repetition, and repetition create a new habit or belief. Miho helped herself cement the new belief in her subconscious in three ways: she spoke or thought the power phrase often, and every time the negative lie that bound her popped up; she made a number of paper copies of the power phrase and put them everywhere she knew she would see them, from her bedside table to the fridge to the dashboard of her car; and she recorded her list of power phrases on her phone, repeating each phrase three times, and then listened to the loop of power phrases before she fell asleep and again when she woke up in the morning when her brain waves were most receptive.

Following those four steps is what it takes to help the grass grow, metaphorically speaking, over a negative belief and for a new, more positive belief to take root in your subconscious.

Now, in case you're thinking, "But I don't have any lies that bind," let me assure you that in the decades I've been doing this work, there has never been a single person I've worked with who didn't have a list of limiting beliefs that were holding them back. Some lists are longer than others. One client I worked with, a handsome and put-together young man who struggled to interview successfully for a job right out of business school, assured me he had no limiting beliefs whatsoever.

"Humor me," I said, "and see if you can maybe jot down a couple of lies that bind for your homework."

At our next session, he wound up handing me a page and a half of single-spaced typed lies that bind, including "Other people are more qualified than you." *No wonder* he was having such a rough time nailing his interviews.

What about you?

How clearly and well do you know thyself as a speaker and communicator?

How specifically are you able to identify your blessings (the unique talents and abilities that make you you) and your blocks (your limiting beliefs and behaviors) as they relate to and influence your three presence planes?

How willing and able are you to pinpoint and reframe your lies that bind?

Your answers to those questions will determine your movement forward as a speaker and presenter and your ability to magnify your Charismatic Presence.

To know thyself is a lifelong process. And if you're going to get up and share your ideas and your wisdom in front of an audience, it's a downright necessity. Because the more you know thyself, the more you can play to your strengths and downplay (or strengthen, through training and commitment) your so-called "weaknesses," which builds up your confidence and Charismatic Presence.

You can't move forward until you have the courage to look in the mirror and see what you've got going for or against you as a speaker and communicator.

You must know thyself, so you can learn to be thyself when the spotlight is on you and it's your time to claim the stage, which is what we'll explore in the next chapter.

Presence Principle One:
Know Thyself

Do A Little Digging. Answer the self-reflection questions in this chapter. What did you learn about your strengths, fears, and challenges that bears exploring more deeply?

Pinpoint Your Lies That Bind. Make a comprehensive list of the limiting beliefs that keep you from feeling confident and capable as a speaker, communicator, and/or leader.

Rate Your Lies That Bind. Give each lie that binds a rating of fear/anxiety from one to five (if one is "almost none" and five is "off the charts"). Which lies that bind challenge you the most (your fours or fives)?

Turn Your Lies That Bind Into Power Phrases. Rephrase your power phrases into more useful, empowering phrases that go to the heart of the matter. Make sure to write them as if they are a done deal, occurring now and not in the future.

Internalize Your Power Phrases. Read, record, listen to, and speak your list of lies that bind daily. Pick a particular power phrase, post twenty copies of it everywhere you can think of, and focus on it for sixty days.

(Bonus) Convince Yourself So You Can Convince Others. If you struggle to believe a power phrase, act like a lawyer: come up with three hard pieces of evidence in your life and work that prove the power phrase is true.

CHAPTER 4

BE THYSELF

Presence Principle Two:
Be Thyself

Truth has energy that touches people.

Barbra Streisand, legendary producer, singer, and actor[17]

Alice, a brilliant, bubbly thirty-something with infectious enthusiasm, was worried about her upcoming interview for a higher-level position at the corporation where she worked as a tech professional. Though she'd been prepping for the interview for days, she felt uncertain about how she would perform.

"Here's the thing," she explained in a torrent of words on our Zoom coaching call, "I've already had two colleagues tell me that I am going to need to tone down who I am to ace this interview. Specifically, they said I need to be less enthusiastic and more reserved, or I won't be taken seriously, especially since I'm younger than the other candidates. They told me that instead of relying on my preparation and trusting myself to be able to think on my feet, which is what I typically do, I need to script out and memorize my responses so I don't go off course in the interview. And I've tried. But it just makes me feel stiff and self-conscious, and like

I'm playing at being someone I'm not. Which is really messing with my confidence."

"Alice," I said, "You are bright, articulate, and more than qualified for this position. You are also a bundle of positive energy with enough enthusiasm for three people. These qualities are core parts of you. If you go into this interview trying to put a lid on them, you're not only going to dishonor yourself; you're going to dishonor the folks who are considering hiring you. They need to be able to see, hear, and feel who you really are so they can decide if the person you are is the person they want for the position."

Alice agreed and committed to showing up as genuinely as possible in the interview. "After all," she said, "I wouldn't want to work for people who wouldn't appreciate the real me."

Shortly after the interview, Alice sent me an exuberant email. "It went really *great*," she wrote. "Thanks for the confidence boost. I left our coaching session ready to bring my full, energetic self to the table, and I think that was a positive approach."

She was right. Because on the heels of that email came another one, brimming with even more enthusiasm: "They're moving me on to the next round. Woo-hoo!"

Alice's interview experience and the ensuing outcome were positive because she was willing to embrace the second principle of Charismatic Presence: Be thyself.

Be Thyself: Charismatic Presence Principle Two

To be thyself means being relaxed and present in the moment at hand, breathing easily, and connecting with your eyes, heart, and soul to others who are watching.

It's a willingness to honor the *sacred stage* (the platform from which you are speaking, whether it's a majestic proscenium theater or a rickety podium in a conference breakout room) by honoring the "sacred eight." The sacred eight is the vocal and energetic figure eight of communication between you and every member of your audience that, as a speaker, is your duty to establish and maintain. To honor the sacred stage and the sacred eight, you must be willing to allow others to see, hear, feel, and know your authentic self.

To be thyself means having the courage to reveal yourself, warts and all, to your audience of one or many. Because the more willing you are to be thyself, the more your audience members can relate to you. As legendary singer, producer, actor, director, and author Barbra Streisand wrote in her memoir *My Name Is Barbra*, ". . . when you have the privilege of being up on stage, raised above the audience, you owe them something more . . . something truthful . . . truth has an energy that touches people."[18] Truth is, there is only one you, and you're meant to be the most you that you can be. Nobody can be you better than you. Or, as my Aunt Ann from Boston used to say, "You *aah* what you *aah*."

That said, being who you *aah*, relaxed and comfortable in the moment while people are watching (especially people you want to impress), can be extremely challenging. If you have ever stressed out and stumbled while trying to accurately type a document, play an instrument, or add up a column of numbers in front of someone who was waiting expectantly for you to finish or *get it right*, you know what I mean.

"Being yourself on a stage is really hard," said my friend, Tom Paxton, ASCAP Lifetime Achievement Award honoree and a folk singer and songwriter with a performing career of sixty-plus years. "When I did my first [solo singing] performances in Oklahoma," he continued, "I had been on the stage as an actor, many, many times, but this was totally different. My knees were literally shaking, and they shook for the first two or three performances in public I ever gave. And my friend, Bob Gibson, explained all of that. He said, 'We're in a business where they put us in front of a microphone that is going to amplify everything we say or do in front of an audience, with chairs all facing us, they shine a light on *only* us—and then they tell us just to be ourselves.'"

Being thyself when eyeballs are on you can be so challenging that many people automatically engage in behaviors that help them feel hidden and protected.

For example, I always see the metaphoric masks go up and the invisible armor clanking into place during group training when I ask attendees to pair up, face each other, and stand in silence, looking into each other's eyes for what can feel like sixty of the longest seconds of their lives. In a flurry of uncomfortable giggles and eye-rolling, their bodies stiffen, and their arms and hands leap into positions that scream, "Stay away. I'm protecting myself":

- *The Coach* (arms folded across their chest)

- *The Favorite Uncle* (hands in pockets, as if rummaging for candy or money to give to the kids, like my Uncle Tom)

- *The Magician* (hands behind the back, as in "Am I holding the card in my left hand or my right hand?")

- *The Opera Singer* (hands clasped at the waist, as if begging)

- *The Fig Leaf* (my favorite, which looks just like it sounds, clasped hands slung low protecting the groin)

It happens every time.

The desire to shield and protect ourselves when feeling vulnerable under public scrutiny stems from our tendency as humans to want to please, impress, be liked, fit in, and be seen as perfect (no matter how unreasonable and unattainable that may be). We are afraid that if we reveal our true selves, we will expose our shameful little secret: That we are, at our core, simply not good enough, especially in comparison to others, and will ultimately be rejected.

The fear of being "cast out" was well founded back in tribal days, when our lives depended on the safety of our fellow tribal members—there is, after all, safety in numbers. Being kicked out of the tribe, for whatever reason, opened us up to life-threatening physical dangers (saber-tooth tigers, wild animals, punishing weather, enemies hiding in the bushes). Those ancient fears are firmly embedded in our DNA and can still hold considerable sway over us, even in modern times.

And so, when faced with an audience (what I call the beast with many heads), which, for many people, is a stressor that is worse than the idea of death, human beings tend to "armor up," freeze, or cut and run. We do everything possible to avoid the moment we're in, hiding behind sanitized, false versions of ourselves, behind masks of our making. We armor up, emotionally speaking, in order to protect ourselves. We refuse to connect eyeball-to-eyeball, heart-to-heart with our audience, talking instead to the slides on the screen or to our feet on the floor. We bury our faces in our notes or read our script word for word. We race through our presentations, wanting to end the torture as quickly as possible. We hold sarcasm up like a sword and shield or speak too quietly or loudly, fending off real connection with others.

Hiding behind a metaphoric mask not only short-circuits our Charismatic Presence and limits our impact as speakers, but it's also downright exhausting.

To make my point, I'd like you to stop what you're doing and hold this book (or the device you're reading it on) out in front of you with one hand, with your arm dead straight.

Good.

Now, keep holding it out in front of you while you count slowly to sixty.

No cheating. Don't put it down. Keep holding that book or device straight out in front of you. Is your arm getting heavier and heavier? No doubt it is.

After sixty seconds, go ahead and put the book or device down. Feels good, huh? What a relief, right?

Well, imagine that the book or device is the mask you potentially wear every day (or when giving presentations) that prevents your authentic self from being seen, heard, or felt. Holding up that mask is hard work. In truth, holding up that mask is harder work than actively being and revealing yourself.

It can be an out-and-out relief to finally show yourself and be yourself. That's what my client, Joe, the director of a state-wide nonprofit program designed to support children and families challenged by addiction, ultimately discovered.

Jay's Story: Taking The Risk To Really Reveal

Jay is a tall and striking medical professional and a person in recovery from substance use disorder for more than thirty years. He had always danced uncomfortably around the line between revealing and not revealing his history of addiction when pitching a nonprofit program he helms that assists families with addiction challenges. In one of our coaching sessions, as we were prepping him for an important talk in front of state legislators, Jay said, "I want the program, and not me, to get the attention. And I worry that if I reveal my own firsthand experience as a person in recovery, it could be distracting. People are always so surprised that a guy who looks and dresses like me, who's in a respected position of leadership, has a history of addiction. What if it causes audience members to turn off and take me less seriously? What if it somehow negatively affects my professional standing?" Then he paused and smiled: "But my addiction story is a huge part of who I am. How can I not share it?"

As we worked on his presentation, Jay experimented with telling his story, including how much of it to share and where it should be placed within the context of his talk. It was obvious to us both that he was more alive and present (and, frankly, quite riveting) when he revealed even a small part of his addiction story. Still, as the speaking date approached, he remained on the fence about whether to share it.

The day of the presentation, Jay decided to step over the line and drop the mask. "Something came over me," he told me afterward, with a mixture of amazement and exultation. "I just decided, *screw it. I need to show up as who I am.* And I shared the fact that I was a person in recovery from opioid and alcohol use disorder and that I understood firsthand the importance of the kind of programming our nonprofit provides. And honestly, I was on fire. I've never been so eloquent and so sure of what I was saying. It was exhilarating and scary but easy, all at the same time. I was in total flow. And when I was done, the State Attorney General herself commended me and asked me to bring my message to the rest of the State. I just don't think that would have happened if I hadn't taken the risk to bring my full self to the moment."

Time and again in my coaching practice, I've heard stories like Jay's from clients who have taken the risk to drop the mask and be themselves with others watching. Whether they've shared, for the first time, images of their personal artwork within the framework of a professional, academic talk or shared a personal story about their own struggles as business owners when lecturing about entrepreneurship, the joy and relief my clients experience when dropping the mask and being real and revealed is palpable. And so does the increased connection and engagement they experience with their audience members. As my clients have learned, when you are willing to be thyself in front of an audience of one or many, your audience members will be more inclined to show up more fully and authentically in return. This is how genuine relationships and audience buy-in are sparked and built.

That said, there is no getting around the fact that taking the risk to drop your mask and reveal who you are on a public platform, or even with another human being, will nudge you right into the murky middle of discomfort.

The Murky Middle Of Discomfort: A Place Of Learning, Growth, And Uncertainty

The murky middle of discomfort is my term for the place of awkwardness and unknowing you must step into if you want to learn and grow. It's the icky limbo space between what you already know and what you don't know yet. Stepping into the murky middle of discomfort requires moving out of your comfort zone—like swimming without your water wings for the very first time, trying out your high school French when ordering dinner in a busy Parisian restaurant, or being the first to say "I love you" when you're dating someone.

I stepped into the murky middle of discomfort in a way that changed me forever when, as a young actor, I performed my very first acting class scene for New York City acting teacher Warren Robertson and an audience of professional acting colleagues. Doing the scene itself was terrifying enough. But receiving Warren's critique afterward, as I stood trembling and expectant under the stage lights, pushed me to places I'd never been before. Here, as quoted from my book, *Touch the Sky! Find Your Voice, Speak Your Truth, Make Your Mark*, is what Warren said:

> "Look at you! You're so striking. You have such presence. We expected so much of you. But instead, you disappointed us ... You didn't so much inhabit the character as you were playing the idea of the character. Which left me wondering, 'Where is Eleni? Who is Eleni? What choices would Eleni make as this character? That's what we're interested in. We're interested in you. In what you think, in what you know, in

what you choose. We don't want to see your idea of this character. We want to see you bring who you are to it."

I am stunned, speechless. Nobody has ever told me they want to see me, the real me, either onstage or off. And how the hell do I actually do that?[19]

Learning "how to do that" became my focus in acting class and on public stages from that moment on. I threw my arms wide and stepped into the murky middle of discomfort again and again. It was both thrilling and excruciating.

A large part of what I learned from the many hours I devoted to my acting training was that who I was and what I brought to the stage was enough, including my so-called "imperfections." The more I allowed myself to bring my truth, vulnerability, and perspective to my acting work, the more comfortable and consistent I became in scripted and unscripted spotlight moments. This freed and fanned the flame of my Charismatic Presence.

I knew what I was learning had taken hold the day I happened to accompany my then-husband, actor Marcus Smythe, to a commercial audition for Prego spaghetti sauce. The actor he was supposed to be paired up with didn't show up, so the casting director asked if I'd step in and read opposite Marcus. Wearing what would be considered the wrong kind of clothes for TV (all black and shapeless), with not a smidgen of makeup on (horrors!), and with unstyled, somewhat dirty hair (yikes!) I jumped into reading the role opposite my husband. I was relaxed, playful, present, and imperfect. I did my best with the material and then just let it go. To my surprise, when the commercial casting director called the house the next day, it was to book me for the job and not Marcus. And all because, instead of trying to impress anyone, I had just spontaneously been me.

That experience reinforced yet again the core lesson of presence principle two: The more relaxed and real we are, the more others can relate to us. Because it's not about perfection, it's about connection—with who we are at our core and with whoever we're engaging with. As I like to say, *messy is connect-y.*

Yeah, Well, And . . .?

"OK," you may be thinking, "that's all fine and good, but how do I, a nonactor and business professional, learn how to be myself in front of an audience without taking an acting class, for Pete's sake?"

Well, to begin with, if you want to be thyself under public scrutiny, you've got to be willing to do three things. Let's start with the first one.

Embrace Who You Are

First and foremost, you must be willing to believe in your inherent value as a human being (warts and all).

Now, I can't make you embrace your yumminess. But I strongly suggest you use your power phrases to bolster yourself from the inside out.

I can also suggest that you create what I call a personal manifesto to help you pinpoint and embrace who you are at your core and what motivates you. Here's how I defined a personal manifesto in my book *Claim the Stage! A Woman's Guild to Speaking Up, Standing Out and Taking Leadership:*

> "A manifesto is a written statement declaring publicly the intentions, motives, or views of the issuer. Relative to the work I do with clients, a personal manifesto is a soul-stirring, written declaration of self as it relates to the specific focus of our work. It is the result of sitting down with your list of blessings and power phrases, holding your heart wide open to the magical juju of the creative muse, and allowing the pen in your hand to declare on paper who you are and what you're here to do."[20]

Below is an edited example of a personal manifesto written by my client, Felix, many moons ago. Felix, a therapist, was on the verge of offering group workshops for men and was anxious about it. He called his manifesto "Public Speaking Heaven" and included several power phrases from his list, which I've italicized:

"I have a message to share with the world. The world is my audience. I am alive. I am strong. I am powerful. I am also loving and gentle. I have something to give you, world. Something to offer. It is a message of hope. A message of love.

I feel confident. Energetic. Relaxed. Free-flowing. Alive. Open. Receptive. There is no pressure. There is joyous sharing with the audience.

I have a message to deliver, and I want to hear from my audience. Good or bad comments, I don't care. I know my truth. I know what I am offering. Some love it, and some hate it. I welcome questions, comments, and critiques. They make me better and smarter.

I am growing. *I am letting go of control.* I have no expectations. No outcome. *I am fully present in the moment.* I am breathing deeply, slowly. I am alive and tingling. I am moving, responding, standing firm, and giving. I am free. I am me. I can be whatever I want to be.

Fear is energy and excitement.

Breathe.

Seize the moment. These people have come to hear me speak.

I inspire. I lead. It is their choice if they follow."

To create a personal manifesto, simply sit down with your lists of blessings and power phrases and consider the totality of what you are working on as a presenter and communicator. Then, put pen to paper (or fingers to your keyboard) and write, without editing. Let your subconscious inform you.

Write in the present tense as if it's a done deal right now—no "I will" or "someday." Trust that whatever you write will be a unique reflection of you. You'll know it's finished, and as it should be, if it lifts you up and stirs your soul when you read it out loud. Then, internalize it by reading it often (aloud, if possible). Print it out, frame it, and put it on your desk. Read it (or record and listen to it) before you step into a spotlight moment. Let it remind you of your worth and of the importance of showing up, stepping up, and speaking up.

Breathe And Be With "Eleni Breaths"

The second step toward being thyself involves learning how to stay breathing, relaxed, and present in the murky middle of discomfort when eyeballs are on you and the pressure to come through is high.

You cannot be thyself in a spotlight moment if you're in a body that is physically tense (or "sphinctered up," as I like to say). That's because you can neither transmit nor receive properly in a body that is armored up or shut down. You can't breathe properly, either. And if you're not breathing, you're not thinking.

I discovered the value of using my breath to release tension in my body in a professional acting class taught by the late and very great acting teacher Michael Howard in New York City. At the start of each class, before we launched into scene work or acting exercises, we laid down as a group on the dusty studio floor and individually did an internal scan of our bodies from head to toe. When we encountered a tense area—our stomach, jaw, or shoulders, for example—we released the tension by exhaling with an audible "aah" (like in a doctor's office).

Sometimes, this breathing and relaxation work released emotion (laughter, tears). Overall, it served to get rid of the physical and emotional armor that we had invariably raised to protect us from the day-to-day challenge of living and working as actors in New York City.

"You can't do the work until you let go of the armor," Michael would say.

This breathwork is a core element of my coaching and training practice.

"Raise your shoulders to your ears," I'll say to a client. "Tense up. Then, when you're ready, lower your shoulders and release with an aah." My clients call these breaths "Eleni breaths."

As I often say, "I don't care what you call them; I just want you to do them."

When it comes to learning how to be present in public, mindfulness breathing is your greatest tool. The simple act of noticing where you're carrying tension in your body and then releasing it with an audible breath can help you be more relaxed and present in the moment at hand—especially in the days and moments leading up to giving a presentation.

Uncover And Share

The third step involves revealing and sharing who you are and what you are feeling with others—especially when it would be easier not to.

This step takes two things: courage and practice.

The word "courage" comes from the French word "*coeur,*" which means "heart." In relation to speaking and to the second presence principle, I view courage as a willingness to speak and share from your heart, even if it's scary.

Some examples of this kind of courage include:

- Allowing tears to fall while giving the toast at your daughter's wedding or giving a eulogy at a funeral.

- Raising your hand in a lecture or a meeting to ask a so-called "silly" or "stupid" question.

- Sharing a personal story when you typically would avoid doing so.

For instance, a client I'll call "Elliot," the head of global training at an international bio-tech company, courageously practiced uncovering and sharing when he told a personal story while giving the kickoff keynote at his company's annual conference. He found it both challenging and extremely rewarding. As he put it, ". . . being myself by revealing personal details about my life on stage was the hardest thing I had to do. It was also the most commented-on aspect of my speech. People thought it was a brave choice, considering not one other person the entire three-day conference did anything remotely similar. The stuff you teach works!"

You can encourage courage by practicing being fully present in situations that are less risky than, say, presenting in front of your boss. Try it at the grocery store with the checkout clerk, for example. Look them in the eye while staying physically relaxed and open, and mean it when you ask, "How are you today?" Then, actively listen to their response. Go a little deeper with your own reply when they ask you a question.

The same holds true with virtual scenarios: Don't fiddle with your phone or answer email when you're in a Zoom meeting or hide behind a static thumbnail photo just because it's safer and easier. Turn on your camera, and allow yourself to be seen, even if your hair isn't perfect. Pay attention when others are talking; speak up and share your perspective, especially when it would be easier not to.

Presence—truly being thyself when others are watching—takes practice. So, practice being present.

Because *presence equals being present.* You can't phone presence in. You've got to be present to create presence.

Think about that for a moment: Presence equals being present.

How willing are you to be present with another human being, unmasked and vulnerable, in the name of being thyself?

How willing are you to simply be, in silence or while talking, radiating who you are, while letting yourself see and be seen by others in a group setting?

How willing are you to embrace all of you—including your so-called imperfections—when others are watching, in the name of honoring presence principle two?

As Dr. Seuss wrote in his children's book, *Happy Birthday to You*:

> *"Today you are You, that is truer than true. There is no one alive who is You-er than You."*[21]

The more willing you are to be you-er than you, the more you will radiate a genuine and magnetic Charismatic Presence. And the greater your presence, the greater your impact—as a speaker, a leader, and a human being.

Presence Principle One:
Know Thyself

Embrace Who You Are. Grab a pen and a piece of paper and write stream-of-consciously (no editing) for ten minutes with the following sentence as your starting point: "When I consider my willingness to believe that I'm valuable just as I am, I realize . . .". What did you learn about yourself?

Write A Personal Manifesto. Using the approach outlined in this chapter, write a personal manifesto that honors the reason you were compelled to buy and read this book. How does it make you feel to read it aloud?

Practice "Eleni Breaths." Get into the habit of checking in with yourself several times a day to diffuse mounting physical tension. Close your eyes, place your hand on your belly, and connect with your breath. Then, pinpoint the areas in your body where you're armored up, like your shoulders. Then, deliberately tense and release those areas while exhaling with an audible "aah."

Practice Uncovering And Sharing. During the course of your day or week, look for opportunities to reveal and share yourself more fully with the people you encounter.

CHAPTER 5

Presence Principle Three:
Prepare Thyself

*Talk about something that you know and know that you know," . . .
"Don't spend ten minutes or ten hours preparing a talk:
spend ten weeks or ten months. Better still, spend ten years."*
ANDREW CARNEGIE[22]

*Amateurs practice until they get it right.
Professionals practice until they can't get it wrong.*
ANONYMOUS

Victor, an affable and brilliant entrepreneur, had just received the prestigious 30 Under 30 award from *Forbes Magazine* for a product he'd invented that could revolutionize the manufacturing industry. At his first presentation coaching meeting with me, he was both incredulous and ecstatic.

"Five minutes," he declared, sinking into my office chair. "That's what *Forbes* has given me to speak at their annual summit next month. I'll be in front of an invited audience of some of the most important business titans in the world, not to mention the media up the wazoo. It's the opportunity of a lifetime. So, I need to do two things: manage my anxiety so it doesn't throw me and create and deliver a five-minute talk people will remember."

"Well," I said, "you can pack a real punch in five minutes if you prepare properly. Let's dive in and put together a talk they'll never forget."

Over the course of two-and-a-half weeks, Victor and I met often, slowly and carefully building his talk. We wanted it to be conversational and relatable and spark potential investors into wanting to know more.

Rehearsing his talk aloud against a stopwatch for the first time, Victor discovered two things: Five minutes went by in a flash, and his talk was two minutes too long. And so, we methodically trimmed and pruned his talk again, and again, and again—not just to better fit the allotted time frame but to give him (and his audience) space to pause and breathe. "What you leave out is as important as what you leave in," I reminded Victor with every careful edit to his text. "And the shorter the talk, the more each word matters."

Once we'd worked out the talk's content to our satisfaction, we turned our attention to how Victor was delivering it. We made choices about what words to linger on and emphasize and what text to move through more quickly. Taking a directorial approach, I reinforced certain rules of thumb to help make his delivery more impactful.

"Silence is powerful," I said. "Instead of rushing right into your talk, do what your favorite teachers did to kick off a class and command attention: Stand in silence for a moment and breathe deeply as you scan the audience with your eyes. It will settle the room, ground you, and encourage your Charismatic Presence to bloom. Make sure to stop moving and plant your feet before you make an important point so it can land without distraction. Once you've made your point, pause for a moment so your audience has space to take it in."

Incorporating my directorial prompts, Victor then focused on rehearsing his talk aloud as often as possible—not only to me, as he stood on the little wooden stage in my office, but to himself while he was driving or doing mundane tasks. He took me seriously when I said, "Amateurs practice until they get it right. Professionals practice until they can't get it wrong."

The more Victor rehearsed his talk, the more it sunk into his subconscious mind. Soon, he knew the talk so well that he became almost bored with it. I knew then he was nearly ready for his big moment.

During our final session, we explored some simple tools and techniques to help him manage any pre-show anxiety or adrenaline that could potentially derail him. "Having a couple of go-to techniques to still your mind, ground your body, and focus your attention is essential," I explained. "They give you something you can control in what can feel like an out-of-control moment." Victor particularly resonated with my F.B.I. (foot, breath, intention) technique: He grounded himself by feeling the ground under his feet, brought his breath under control by inhaling and exhaling deeply seven to ten times, and then reminded himself of his intention—what he was there to do in relationship to the audience. I also suggested to Victor that he pinpoint a brief mantra or short empowering phrase, like "I've got this," "I'm nervous and excited," or "I'm relaxed and ready," that he could think or say to himself prior to stepping into his upcoming spotlight moment. These pre-show prep techniques made Victor feel even more confident and ready to give his presentation than he already was.

This is why, on the day Victor's talk arrived, I wasn't remotely surprised to get his text telling me it had gone like gangbusters. In fact, Victor's five-minute talk had packed such a powerful punch that he had to stay an extra day at the summit venue to accommodate all the meeting requests from intrigued investors and business owners. Mission accomplished.

Victor met his goals as a presenter because he had put in the work. With every fiber of his being, he had embraced the third principle of Charismatic Presence: Prepare thyself.

Prepare Thyself: The Third Principle Of Charismatic Presence

Principle three underscores what is perhaps the single greatest differentiator between peak performers and those who fall short of their potential as speakers: the willingness to do what it takes to be thoroughly prepared for your spotlight moments.

I am a proud preparation zealot, largely due to my training as an actor. I was taught to believe that the stage (whether it's a proscenium theater, a conference podium, or a rectangle on Zoom) is a sacred space and that you honor it by coming to it as prepared as possible.

As Victor discovered (and embodied) in the coaching sessions leading to his speaking event, preparation *involves making choices about the material itself and then practicing it* so that it becomes a part of your subconscious mind. The more you internalize the material, the freer you are to be present in the moment, which kicks your Charismatic Presence into higher gear.

Preparation also involves *maximizing your verbal and physical presence* by warming up your voice and body so that you can be physically and vocally relaxed, responsive, and fluid.

Finally, preparation involves *amping up your energetic presence by getting your head in the game*. This means learning how to manage preshow jitters brought on by your little nay-saying inner judges Moe and Schmoe. Because how you think (and speak to yourself) before you step into a spotlight moment will determine your performance.

The more you prepare, the more comfortable, confident, and consistent you can be under pressure and the more Charismatic Presence you will generate. This is true whether you're speaking for an hour or for five minutes.

To Ace Your Talk, Prepare Like An Actor

Victor prepared for his speaking engagement the way actors prepare for a theater production or a role in a movie. They do everything in their power to feel ready, giving themselves as much time as possible to muse about the material and make the strongest delivery choices.

Actors (and speakers) also learn to control whatever elements are within their control in the days, hours, and minutes leading up to showtime. Because they know that once the curtain goes up, all kinds of things that are outside of their control can occur. Like a cockroach the size of Mars, walking across the stage in full view of the audience while you're spouting your biggest, bestest monologue; or the projector blowing up and your PowerPoint suddenly going bye-bye. Or, a person in the front row deciding to slowly inch their way to the restroom using their walker right when you're getting to the good stuff. All those things happened to me, either as an actor or as a speaker. Each time, I was very glad I'd done the work to internalize my lines or my presentation so I could dance with what I was given and not let the unexpected throw me.

That sense of security around the material is why actors are so nutty about preparation in general and rehearsal in particular. If you have ever been in a theater production (even if you only played a tree in your fifth-grade holiday pageant), you will remember that you rehearsed for many hours and days just to be ready for an hour- or two-hour-long performance. The fact is, for peak performance, the ratio of preparation (rehearsal) to performance averages one-and-a-half hours of rehearsal for every minute of performance time. This is why professional actors will typically rehearse a two-hour play for one month, six days a week, eight hours a day (except for the last week or so, when the Actor's Equity Association union allows them to rehearse ten out of twelve hours a day).

Without those specific parameters around rehearsal time and expectations around what needs to be set in stone and by when, most professional actors would do what most regular people do when it comes to prepping presentations: procrastinate on making choices around the material and memorizing or internalizing it.

It has been said that mastery-level ability in any discipline involves ten thousand hours of practice. This is why when asked in an interview what her practice schedule was like as a child and young music student, internationally known jazz artist and saxophone master Alexa Tarantino replied, "Four hours every day after school, and eight to ten hours a day in Conservatory."[23]

It takes discipline, focus, strategy, and time to be prepared enough to be confident and present under pressure, but the rewards are enormous. Let's break down the elements of preparation and when to engage in them.

The Two Phases Of Preparation: Preshow And Showtime

My experience as an actor and speaker has taught me that there are two phases of preparation: preshow and showtime. Each phase involves specific components—steps taken at specific times for specific reasons.

Phase One—Preshow

This first phase involves the weeks and days leading up to the morning of the day when you will be delivering your speech, pitch, or presentation. This phase focuses on laying down a solid presentation framework to explore, select, and rehearse the stickiest content and delivery choices possible. The more you commit to making the most of this phase, the more confident you'll be, and the more you'll be able to surrender to the stage when the proverbial curtain goes up.

Here are the elements of the preshow phase:

Creating a production schedule. For an actor, day one of rehearsal always involves being handed not only a script but a detailed rehearsal schedule determined by the director. This production schedule gives actors a playing field, with parameters in which to create and ultimately finesse their work. I can't encourage you enough to think like an actor (and perhaps a director) and get in the habit of creating and honoring a production schedule for yourself. Working backward from the date of your speaking engagement, determine:

- Specific dates and times during which you intend to brainstorm, shape, and finesse the material (put them in your calendar and honor them).

- A date by which the written material needs to be set in stone (slides included) so you can begin to practice it aloud.

- A date by which you need to be "off book" (meaning you let go of the need to read or rely heavily on your notes as you speak).

- A date (or dates) on which you have a full "dress rehearsal" with slides and props and in the wardrobe (shoes included) you intend to wear.

Once you've determined the framework of the production schedule, here are some of the things you might choose to do within its parameters:

Determine the presentation logistics. By logistics, I mean such things as the location of the speaking event, the number of audience members who will be present, the room setup, and available/planned audiovisual equipment. If presenting on a virtual platform, determine which platform (e.g., Zoom, Microsoft Teams), what you will need to create and convey in advance to the host (e.g., poll questions), and when you will be able to meet with them prior to the event for a tech rehearsal.

Create a speaker vision statement (more on this in chapter 7), record it on your phone and listen to it repeatedly.

Structure and build your presentation. For specific tools to help you position, outline, and flesh out both a long-form and short-form presentation, see chapter 9.

Create slides if needed. Remember that slides are simply a choice of content designed to support you, the star of the show. Sometimes, you don't even need slides at all.

Determine the system of notes you'll be using for both rehearsal and delivery (and by that, I do *not* mean using your PowerPoint slides as a repository for copious, bulleted notes).

Gather your tech and your props (e.g., a slide advancer, handheld notes) that support your presentation. Work with them as you rehearse so that using them becomes second nature to you.

Determine presentation wardrobe and make repairs and adjustments (e.g., rough up the soles of slippery shoes, tighten straps that tend to slip, check out how your shirt looks on Zoom to make sure the print isn't too busy for the camera, or that it doesn't bunch up when you sit).

Practice, practice, practice! The more you rehearse, the more you internalize your presentation. The more you internalize your presentation, the more you can relax into the moment and embody your Charismatic Presence.

To make rehearsing less overwhelming, break your presentation into chunks and rehearse aloud, one chunk at a time. As my friend, Steve Swavely, PhD, CCP, author of *Ignite Your Leadership: The Power of Neuropsychology to Optimize Team Performance*,[24] once said to me, "Chunking is a proven way to increase memory capacity. Rehearsing out loud gives our brain an extra set of data (audio data) to help build the memory."

Next, begin to string a couple of chunks together and rehearse these longer chunks until you get to the point that you're ready to string all the chunks together. Practice while doing "mindless" tasks, like vacuuming, walking, or driving. As Steve Swavely further explains, "Practicing while doing mindless tasks helps move the material from the thinking system to the autopilot (memory) system for later use."

The more you practice, the more the material sinks into your subconscious, creating new neural pathways. Brain specialist and former president of the National Speakers Association, John B. Molidor, puts it perfectly: "Practice makes habit."

Phase Two—Showtime

This phase begins the morning of the speaking event—from the moment when you wake up, think, "OMG. Today's the day," and immediately start to sphincter up. It continues up until the moment you open your mouth and begin to deliver your talk.

Showtime is by far the trickiest part for my clients to manage, even for clients who have thoroughly prepared and rehearsed, like Victor. That's why the focus of this phase needs to be on controlling whatever elements you can so you can feel centered, relaxed, and ready when the metaphorical curtain rises.

There are three parts to showtime prep:

1. Before you get to the speaking venue

2. Once you arrive at the venue

3. When you're "on deck" waiting to go on.

Let's look at what you can do to help yourself stay grounded and out of the reach of your inner judges, Moe and Schmoe, during each of these preshow prep segments:

1. Before You Arrive At The Venue:

Warm up your voice with vocal exercises, like humming any old melody; blowing through relaxed, pursed lips like a baby blowing spit bubbles; running quickly through your material aloud (this is called a speed-through). A good time to do this is in the shower or in the car on the way to the gig. Or put on your favorite music and sing along. Rapidly repeating tongue twisters like "red leather, yellow leather" is also a good way to relax your jaw and dust the cobwebs off your voice. A client of mine loves to warm up his voice before a talk by reading some pages aloud from his little girl's favorite Dr. Seuss book, *Fox in Sox*, which is written entirely in rhymed tongue twisters.

Warm up your body. Get your physical presence plane ready for action by going for a run or a workout. Take a brisk walk around the building. Do a few push-ups, stretches, or a little yoga or tai chi—whatever works for you and gets your blood flowing. Warming up your body wakes up your whole being. As Annie-B Parson, the esteemed choreographer of David Byrne and Fatboy Slim's *Here Lies Love* Broadway musical, said, ". . . when you engage the body, you also engage the mind and the heart."[25]

Dress in your speaking wardrobe, checking for comfort and breathability. Eliminate jangly jewelry or coins in your pocket (though most of us aren't carrying those anymore). Check once more that you're not wearing anything that might slip, rip, or distract (including the zipper in your pants, please—if not, audience members will stop listening while they whisper, point, and crane their necks trying to catch glimpses of your tighty-whities).

Make a list and check it twice. Do a last-minute dummy check to ensure you have everything you need from a computer and tech standpoint. This includes all cords, dongles (who came up with that word?), slide advancer, and audience handouts or giveaways. And don't forget to take a thumb drive with a backup of your slide deck. (For even greater peace of mind, back up your presentation to the cloud and bring a printed copy, just in case).

Leave for the venue early if presenting live in person, with enough time to get lost or deal with last-minute traffic issues. I always fly in a day early or drive to an early-morning speaking engagement the night before, so I can wake up at the venue hotel rested and ready without having had to deal with traffic or weather snafus. If speaking virtually, clear your calendar for the hour before showtime.

2. Once You Arrive At The Venue:

Get to the stage area *(or the boardroom or the conference room) an hour before guests arrive.* If presenting virtually, log in thirty minutes before the start time.

Do a sound, microphone, and tech check. Ensure you know how to turn your mic on and off and that the batteries are fully loaded. Note any feedback hot spot on the stage or speaking area triggered by speakers located in the ceiling. For virtual presentations, ensure your camera, mic, and wi-fi are working properly and your slide deck is loaded and ready to share.

Set the stage. Check to see that all your tools and props are where they need to be, including your computer, stool, notes, handheld visual aids, and capped water bottle (avoid water glasses that could spill, especially ones with ice). If you're presenting virtually, straighten up your desk area to minimize distraction, and set up your notes and prompts so that they are easy to reach and read.

3. When You're On Deck, Waiting To Go On:

I told you about my client, Victor, and his triumphant delivery of the five-minute talk he gave at the *Forbes* summit. What I didn't tell you is that Victor made a whispered cell phone call to me while he was waiting in the wings, a few moments before he stepped up to the podium and into the spotlight in front of an audience of national news media, business titans, and influencers. The call went something like this:

Victor: "It's almost time to go on! Can you hear the buzz out there? Oh my God, I'm so excited and a little nervous, I'm not gonna lie."

Me: "If you weren't feeling a little nervous, I'd think there'd be something wrong with you, Victor. It's totally normal. Have you been doing your deep breathing and grounding work?"

Victor: "Yeah, I'm doing the foot, breath, intention thing you taught me and it's really helping."

Me: "Are you repeating your preshow mantra?"

Victor: "Yeah, I'm saying 'I'm relaxed and ready' over and over to myself, and I'm actually starting to believe it!"

Me: "Good! You're doing everything right. You've got this, Victor."

Victor: "They're calling for me; I've gotta go!"

And just like that, he was whisked to the stage, where, as you remember, he knocked his talk into nosebleed territory.

I bring up this little scenario because it illustrates a hard truth: the moments when you're on deck, right before you step into the spotlight (or the Zoom thumbnail), are by far the trickiest ones to manage in the preparation process.

Here's what you can do to stay calm, centered, and ready in this final preparation phase:

Wake up your physical presence plane.
Standing idly, sitting, and waiting can lock your body down. Counteract this tendency by continuously tensing and releasing the areas of your body most prone to armoring up, like your shoulders, jaw, and hands.

A few minutes before you hit the stage, stand like a king or queen, with your feet slightly apart, your head held high (as if it's being pulled up by a string from its crown) and your shoulders back (as if the center of your chest is being tugged outward by a string).

Then, place your hands on your waist like Superman or Wonder Woman in an expansive, open stance that social psychologist and best-selling author Amy Cuddy calls a power pose. According to Ms. Cuddy, who did groundbreaking research (and a fabulous TED Talk) on postural feedback (or power poses), how you hold your body influences how you feel and behave. Simply put, if you stand in a power pose for three to four minutes, your body tells your brain that you are confident. And the more confident you feel, the more Charismatic Presence you exude.[26]

Prepare your head and maximize your energetic presence with R&R&R.
I'm sure you'll agree that your inner judgers, Moe and Schmoe, are at their worst right in those vulnerable moments just before you take the stage. That's when they ratchet up their efforts to throw you off your game by pummeling you with lies that bind. The louder Moe and Schmoe get, the more your energetic presence plane (and your Charismatic Presence) gets diminished.

To prevent Moe and Schmoe from undermining you and to radiate your most confident, consistent, Charismatic Presence in what can feel like an out-of-control moment, you must engage in activities you can control. Why? Because *fear cannot stop a moving target, action trumps fear.* Engaging in small, repeatable acts like mindfulness breathing, or speaking a prayer or mantra, is what we humans do to self-soothe (much like when we sucked our thumbs when we were little). I call these soothing and centering preshow activities ritual, routine, and repetition, or R&R&R (which is what I reminded Victor to engage in while he was waiting).

In scientific lingo, R&R&R are selected and consistently implemented activities that trigger parasympathetic responses. They are designed to manage an out-of-control sympathetic response to a perceived stressor (like speaking in public). In simple English, R&R&R triggers your body to relax after a period of stress and danger so you can focus your mind, calm and energize your body, get your voice ready for action, and be more present.[27]

A Few Tried-And-True Examples Of R&R&R:

- Speaking or writing your intention (purpose) for the presentation.
- Muttering affirming mantras or power phrases like "I'm nervous and excited," "I'm relaxed and ready," or "I've got this." (FYI, to stay focused and calm, I used to write out my power phrases over and over in a small notebook while I was sitting and waiting to go into auditions as a young actor.)
- Listening to a recording of your speaker vision. (You'll learn what that is and how to write one in chapter 7, and there's an example in appendix B.)
- Invoking guidance from a higher power.
- Silently dedicating your performance to someone you care about ("Ma, this one's for you!").
- Looking at, wearing, or touching a sacred object (e.g., a ring your favorite auntie gave you, a photo of your kids, your good luck socks).

- Shaking the tension out of your body (I call this "getting the yayas out").
- Practicing F.B.I. (foot, breath, intention): ground yourself, bring your breath into your belly, and remember what you're there to do.

I swear by R&R&R, and so do top-level peak performers. For example, singer and recording artist and thirty-two-time Grammy winner Beyoncé has been known to say a prayer with the members of her band before taking the stage. And then there's competitive swimmer Michael Phelps, the winner of twenty-three Olympic gold medals, who I consider to be the poster child for R&R&R. Among the numerous preswim rituals he engages in are listening to hard-core hip-hop (very specific songs that make him feel a very specific way), wiping the starting block with a towel from left to right, and, once he climbs onto that block, crossing his arms and slapping his back with his hands three times.

What's the best R&R&R for you? Whatever works to still your mind gives you comfort and fills you with confidence. When it comes to R&R&R, there's no right or wrong. If it takes sipping from a container of water that you call diva juice when you need a shot of courage, or putting golf balls over and over into a cup before stepping onto the stage, then go for it.

Preparation—in the form of building and practicing your presentation and implementing R&R&R to manage preperformance anxiety—is key to staying out of your head and in the moment. The more in the moment you are, the more your Charismatic Presence can flow and the more you can connect with your audience.

When it comes down to it, preparation is a game changer. So, the question becomes, will you commit to doing it? Or will you not?

Bonus: The First Three Minutes

The first three minutes of your presentation are a critical time to establish the connection between you and your audience. Remember to *connect first* (with your eyes and heart) and *speak second*. This means starting in silence like your best teachers did, grounding yourself, and gathering the attention of your audience. To help the silent moment pass in an active manner, consider thinking a phrase that takes about three to five seconds to complete, like: "I've worked hard on preparing this talk for you, and I'm excited to share it."

So, What About You? Will You Choose To Prepare? Or Will You Shirk The Work?

Most people understand, at least theoretically, the value of preparation. It's why almost every single time I ask members of my training audience, "When are you most confident as a presenter?" they respond with some variation of "When I am prepared and feel like I have a strong grasp of the material."

Yet, when I ask, "How well prepared do you tend to be when you give presentations?" The response typically is, "Not as prepared as I could be."

I follow by asking, "How many of you practice your presentation aloud?" Typically, very few hands wave in the air.

When I prod a bit further as to why they don't take the time to thoroughly prepare their material or rehearse their presentations, here's what the members of my training audience tell me:

"It's too hard."

"I'm too busy."

"I'm a procrastinator."

"It reminds me too much of actually giving the presentation, which is scary."

To this, I say preparation is a choice: you either do it or you don't.

Shirking the work to fully prepare and practice has consequences, not the least of which is diminished confidence, which leads to a diminished Charismatic Presence.

Practice builds confidence.

Confidence builds presence.

And presence is power.

Those are my words. I believe in them so deeply, I had them printed and glued to my office wall.

> *Practice builds confidence.*
> *Confidence builds presence.*
> *And presence is power.*

As my client, Mike, so beautifully put it:

"I had a fear of public speaking. And I still do. But I've learned to lean into it in the name of learning and improving. And so, when there's an opportunity to do it, I put my hand up first. Because even if it scares the hell out of me, I make up for the fear with preparation."

If you really want to become a masterful, charismatic speaker, you must be willing to honor the third principle of Charismatic Presence and prepare thyself by making practicing an integral part of your presentation preparation. And do it *until you can't get it wrong.*

Don't shirk the work. Embrace preparation with everything you've got. Because, as you'll learn in the next chapter, that precious preparation time will invariably come to a screeching halt once the curtain rises.

Presence Principle Three:
Prepare Thyself

Create A Production Schedule. How many days ahead of your performance do you want it to encompass? What milestones (e.g., script finished, slides completed, rehearsal time) do you want it to include? Put those milestones in ink in your calendar and honor them.

Make A Preshow Checklist. What do you need to do or take with you before you leave for your speaking venue? Write it down. Make checking off this list a habit before leaving for any speaking engagement or stepping into a virtual one. The more you do, the more in control you'll feel and the more Charismatic Presence you'll radiate.

Check Your Tech. When you arrive at the venue, get to know your microphone. Determine the ideal sound level, and make sure the mic batteries are full. Run through your slides and familiarize yourself with your slide advancer.

Set The Stage. Make sure any props, notes, or tools are placed exactly where you need them and that the stage area (including your desk) is clear of anything that could distract you or get in your way.

Determine Your On-Deck R&R&R. Choose three repeatable actions that you can engage in that help you stay focused, relaxed, and present and that wake up your three presence planes. Then do them regularly, before every presentation.

CHAPTER 6

COMMIT THYSELF

Presence Principle Four:
Commit Thyself

Commitment: Either you do, or you don't;
there is no in-between.
UNKNOWN

Commitment is an act, not a word.
JEAN-PAUL SARTRE

"**F**irst, it takes your money.

"Then it takes your freedom.

"Then it takes your life."

The words were raw, bare, and gritty with feeling. Behind him, pale, still, tattooed, and in a brown wooden casket, lay his son, Andy. Dead at twenty-four from a two-year dance with heroin.

The mourners—snuffling, sobbing, shifting—listened, devastated but rapt. The man's wife and four daughters huddled an arm's length away, propping each other up with trembling shoulders.

The father pointed to the young people facing him, his son's childhood friends, newly minted adults squirming in unfamiliar suits and ties, sitting puffy-eyed and shock-stunned on hard folding chairs. "I left this casket open so you could see for yourself what drug addiction can do."

"Don't let Andy die in vain!" he said. "Don't let him die in vain! Take a stand in his memory! It's up to you; it's up to all of us, every member of this community, to stop the drug dealers from killing our kids."

Choking on a sob, he paused, his grief laid bare in front of us. Then he walked, unsteadily, to the casket and, for a long, heartbreaking moment, laid a hand on his son's unlined forehead.

Then, he pivoted and faced us, his eyes fierce: "Tomorrow morning, the sun will come up again. And you will be there to see it." He was silent for a moment, the unspoken statement filling the room: "But Andy will not."

His voice now rose and took hold, half plea, half command, like a preacher or a general calling us to action: "As you move forward in your lives, let Andy's death be a signpost, a turning point, a symbol for the moment you decided to take charge of your life and make yourself a better person." Vulnerable, challenging, and impassioned, he was convincing and compelling beyond measure.

Afterward, standing outside the funeral home, we blinked in the midday sun and collectively exhaled the weight of our emotions. A perfect spring day materialized around us in all its bee-buzzing, grass-green glory. My stepson lit a cigarette with a shaky hand and unbuttoned the tight collar of his dress shirt. We stood largely silent; after that eulogy, there really wasn't much more to say. But, it seemed there was certainly a lot left to do in Andy's name.

Though more than a decade has passed since that terrible day, I have never forgotten Andy's father's powerful, emotionally drenched words (or, of course, dear Andy). Because, like the greatest of the world's preachers, teachers, politicians, public speakers, actors, and leaders, he had stood in the full expression of his Charismatic Presence, speaking words to touch our souls, stir our feelings, and inspire action.

Andy's dad had been relentless in his commitment to honor his son's memory by charging us to "stop the drug dealers from killing our kids!" He let nothing—not his fathomless sadness, not the vulnerability of the audience hanging on his words, not the tears that had temporarily choked and silenced him—stop him from honoring that driving, passionate purpose.

That full-on dedication to holding onto what you're there to do in service to the audience, no matter what obstacles get in the way, is the core of the fourth principle of Charismatic Presence: Commit thyself.

Commit Thyself: Presence Principle Four

If you want to fan the flame of your Charismatic Presence and achieve performance mastery, you must be willing to commit yourself to three things: working with a strong intention, relentlessly connecting with your audience, and making bold choices. Let's briefly examine these commitments one by one.

Commit To Working With A Strong Intention

Remember when you first learned to swim? There came a moment when you were tasked with letting go of the side of the pool and trying out the swimming strokes you'd learned. For most of us, that was a scary moment.

To let go of the side of the pool, the desire to swim had to be stronger than the desire to stay safe. Put another way, the *intention* to let go had to be stronger than the intention to cling to the pool's edge.

From a public speaking standpoint, your intention is *to be in service to your audience*, and, just like letting go of the side of the pool, you must be willing to let go of all other distractions (like fear of messing up or wondering if the guy in the second row is asleep) and focus fully on honoring your intention.

Your intention is the *directive* of your presentation, the *why* that motivates you. For example:

- My intention is to convince you of the value of learning and using the new software now, so you can save time and money.

- My intention is to inspire you to think like an actor so you can be more relaxed, real, and relatable when you speak in public (this intention is what drives my Think Like An Actor, Speak Like A Pro training).

- My intention is to change your perspective on filling your calendar so you have more time, energy, and joy.

As a speaker, your job is to define your intention and then hold onto it like a dog with a bone so you can be of the greatest value to your audience. A strong intention can keep you from getting mired in tough, murky, middle moments of discomfort—like when you forget what you intended to say and fear overtakes you, or when you're thrown by a question flung at you by a prospective client, or when strong emotion threatens to derail you, *as occurred with Andy's father*. When you commit to solving your intention, what you're there to do in service to your audience above everything else—*fear, distraction, or discomfort be damned!*—you can surrender to the stage and be truly impactful.

Powerhouse singer Barbra Streisand understood the power of a strong intention when, despite severe performance anxiety that ordinarily kept her from singing in public, she chose to sing a song live, in person, when accepting the Commitment to Life Award from the AIDS Project Los Angeles at a benefit to support victims of the AIDS virus. As she put it,

"I . . . sang live that night. I had to because I realized my own fears about performing live were petty compared to the need to raise money to fight this disease."[28]

Commit To Connecting Relentlessly With Your Audience, Eyeball-To-Eyeball, Heart-To-Heart

This means never letting up on maintaining the sacred eight, the figure eight of connection between you and each member of your audience that I talked about in chapter 4. *Andy's dad did just that, looking us in the eye, talking with us directly, and maintaining that personal, heart-based connection from start to finish. Without this connection, your message is worthless.*

Commit To Making Bold Choices

Choose, and then fully embrace, the strongest, most impactful ways of conveying your message. And don't back off when you convey them.

Whenever I teach this principle, I raise a little sign with "Wishy-Washy" imprinted and circled in red with a red line slashing through. "Ban wishy-washy!" I command. Because as my acting mentor and professor from Brown University, the late and extremely great James O. Barnhill, used to say, "Beige doesn't read from the stage." The stronger and clearer the choices you make about your material, the easier it is for your audience to connect with it. This holds true in both scripted and unscripted moments (we'll talk about the latter in a little bit).

Andy's father demonstrated this principle by doing such things as resting his hand dramatically on his son's forehead as he stood in silence and by deliberately using strong, almost shocking language backing his strong verbal challenge to get us to take action to save lives. "Tomorrow morning, the sun will come up again. And you will be there to see it," he said, then paused. "But Andy will not." We clearly knew where he stood, which is what we hope and expect from any speaker—whether she is delivering a eulogy, a breakout session, or an after-dinner keynote.

The fourth presence principle, commit thyself (to a strong intention, to connecting with your audience, to making bold choices), is particularly useful when you need to think on your feet in an unscripted situation—such as being asked a question you can't answer while your boss is watching or trying to remember what you were going to say next when your PowerPoint malfunctions and you forget to bring your paper notes.

If the idea of having to manage an unscripted moment while eyes are on you makes you sweat, you are not alone. Almost every executive who reaches out to me for coaching has confided in me that they feel more comfortable speaking in public when they have time to prepare and far (far, far) less comfortable having to speak on the fly.

Flying By The Seat Of Your Pants: Improvisation 101

While many people live in fear of unscripted public speaking moments, there are those who live for unscripted moments because they see them as opportunities to make lemonade out of lemons.

This was demonstrated to me by one of the greatest actors of my generation, Jeff Daniels. Jeff is a fellow Michigander who has won multiple acting awards: five Primetime Emmy nominations including two Emmy wins for his brilliant work on the television shows *Godless* and *The Newsroom*, three Tony nominations, including for *To Kill a Mockingbird* on Broadway, and Golden Globe Award nominations for his starring roles in major motion pictures like *The Squid and the Whale*.

I have the good fortune of knowing Jeff through my husband, Jim Fleming, a talent agent who handles Jeff's bookings as a singer-songwriter (yes, Jeff is brilliant at that, too; and did I mention he's also an award-winning playwright?). And so, when Jeff was cast in a Broadway production of *God of Carnage* with three other top-of-the-line actors, including James Gandolfini of *The Sopranos*, my husband and I decided to travel to New York to see it.

As the play—a comedy—unfolded, the phone on the stage rang. James Gandolfini picked up the receiver and had a short conversation with what we understood to be the mother of the character he was playing. Once he was done with the call, he hung up the phone and went on with the scene. A few minutes later, the phone rang again; once again, it was his character's mother, and once again, Mr. Gandolfini spoke a few terse words to her and slammed down the phone. Only this time, the phone slid off its cradle, fell into an open drawer, and the drawer was inadvertently slammed shut. This occurred without Mr. Gandolfini, his fellow actors, or the audience noticing it. The play continued. Ten minutes later, the phone rang again.

Ring ring.

Ring ring.

Ring ring.

Mr. Gandolfini walked over to the table where the phone was supposed to be and stopped in his tracks. His face said it all: "Where's the damn phone?"

The phone kept on ringing.

Ring ring.

Ring ring.

The play couldn't continue until the phone was discovered, and so it ground to an awkward halt. The audience, my hubby and me included, started to whisper and then to giggle. Two actors on stage, Hope Davis and Marcia Gay Harden, started to giggle. Then James Gandolfini started to giggle (which, considering what a mountain of a man he was, was quite the spectacle). He started to giggle so much that he had to turn his back to the audience. As soon we saw his shoulders jiggling up and down in time to his giggles, we laughed louder. The only person not laughing on that stage was Jeff Daniels, who happened to be sitting on the floor in front of the table where the phone was supposed to be.

The phone rang yet again.

Ring ring.

Ring ring.

Jeff suddenly threw his shoulders back and raised his head. His eyes snapped to the drawer in the table he was sitting against. In one fluid motion, he yanked the drawer open, reached inside, and then leaped to his feet. In his hand was the phone. He raised his arm high in a triumphant "Ta-da" gesture, and the audience went crazy, whooping and hollering. And then, not yet done with his impromptu moment, Jeff took a very elaborate bow. The audience jumped to its feet in a spontaneous standing ovation. Finally, Jeff formally handed the phone over to a grinning (and grateful) James Gandolfini, and the play resumed.

When we met Jeff at the stage door after the performance, the very first thing he said to us was, "Wasn't that thing with the phone incredible? It was the most real, most exciting part of the show!"

Jeff was right. That unexpected need to manage the challenge of the missing phone had been as thrilling for the audience to watch as it had been for the actors to manage. It was about as real as real could get, and we hung on every second, breathless with anticipation, wondering, "What in heaven's name is going to happen next?" The actors' vulnerability in that very human moment allowed us to connect with them even more; we were just as invested as they were in how the problem might be solved, allowing us to feel like an essential part of the action. That's the magic of an unscripted moment unspooling right in front of your audience.

Now, you might be thinking, "Yeah, well, professional actors like Jeff Daniels are trained to deal with unexpected moments like that. He knows how to improvise. He probably even likes it. I'm just your average human; what do I know about dealing with that sort of out-of-left-field impromptu moment? I get all tongue-tied just having to answer an unexpected question at a board meeting, for Pete's sake."

Well, what if I told you that you do know a ton about improvising? What if I went even further than that and said *you are a master improviser*?

You Are A Master Improviser. Yes, Really.

Human beings are master improvisers. Every single day, we wake up and improvise our way through whatever is presented to us, one moment at a time.

Our kid wants cereal for breakfast, and the box is empty: improv time.

Our new next-door neighbor unexpectedly knocks on our door, wanting to introduce themselves right when we're getting dressed to go out: improv time (FYI, conversations are always improvised, pulled out of the ether moment by moment).

Traffic on the highway is stuck and stalled for miles, and you have an important presentation to deliver in less than an hour: improv time.

From the moment you wake up to the moment you drift off to sleep at night, you are constantly having to make quick, smart choices about what to say and do. That's improvisation.

As a kid, you improvised all the time when you played with your pals. "Let's play spaceship," your bestie would holler. "I'll be the spaceship commander."

"I'll be the alien monster," you yelled back. And off you went, diving into the game (and the moment) with no hesitation, making stuff up with great enthusiasm and conviction ("Orange M&M's can make me invisible."), your Charismatic Presence at maximum output. You simply gave yourself over to playing freely in the moment.

The willingness and ability to play, to dance with what we're given, to bring the silly and the fun, is what turns a potentially scary, unscripted moment into a space for opportunity and exploration.

Eleni's "Rules" Of Improvisation (And, Well, Life)

That said, "Improv takes self-control and restraint." Alexa Tarantino spoke those words in an interview at the Grand Hotel on Mackinac Island on Labor Day weekend in 2023, where she was headlining a jazz festival.[29] As a noted saxophone player, Alexa knows a whole lot about improvising musically within the context of a song. Like all jazz artists, it's clear to her that you've got to learn the notes before you can "swing" or noodle around musically. The fact is, improvisation has rules and regulations, boundaries within which you are free to play.

When I am working with an individual or a group with the goal of helping their inner improviser come out and play, here are the rules and regulations I share with them:

Say "yes, and . . .." This is the quintessential rule of improv. It means take whatever is presented to you and go with it (grab it and go, as I like to say). Resist the urge to get defensive or to shut someone down (a no-no behavior I call "lidding"). Instead, stay open to—and build upon—the possibilities that the conversation and the moment offer you. To quote actor, comedian, writer, and producer Tina Fey, the creator and star of the TV series *60 Rock* and cast member and head writer of the NBC sketch comedy series *Saturday Night Live* from 1997-2005, "Just say yes and you'll figure it out afterward."[30]

For example, when an actor pal of mine realized the pant zipper of his too-tight, white Elvis costume had suddenly broken open, offering up a rather shocking frontal view of his undies to his audience, he had two choices: to run off the stage in embarrassment or to do a hilarious, five-minute unscripted riff on the broken zipper. He gleefully chose the latter, which brought the house down.

Go with what you know. I like to imagine that each of us is carrying around an invisible box with our name on it, filled with everything we've learned and experienced up to the current moment we're in. In an impromptu moment, you get to rummage around in the box and pull out a nugget of wisdom that befits the situation. For example, suppose someone asks you what Brazil's greatest export is. In that case, you might reply, "tiny thong bikinis," and tell the story of your awesome Brazilian college pal who stopped traffic every spring sunbathing on the lawn of the quad in a suit the size of a postage stamp that, she explained, "was lots bigger than what most Brazilian women wear."

Whatever you pull out of your answer box is good enough—after all, all you can know is what you know right now. And what you know is just fine. It might help to remember that, when it comes to impromptu speaking, the bar is a lot lower, from an audience expectation standpoint, than it might be for a planned, scripted presentation.

Make bold choices. This element of presence principle four is critical to improvisation excellence. It means making the strongest, stickiest choices you can make about what to say and do and then not second-guessing those choices. You exude confidence and feel more confident (which boosts your Charismatic Presence) when you metaphorically plant your flag with surety in a comment or action. Bold choices make moments memorable—so ban wishy-washy. Simply put: Say it, do it, mean it!

Stay ready for what's next. Think like a basketball player; all senses are ready for the next pass or the next play. Stay physically relaxed and present, watching and listening for whatever helpful, important information you can catch and apply. I'm convinced this hyperawareness and openness to the moment is what allowed Jeff Daniels to realize where the "lost" phone was hidden.

Just dive in. This rule of improv reflects the essence of the fourth presence principle, commit thyself: Commit to leaping into the moment *now*, with passion and abandon, the way you did when you were a kid. Leaping in means not allowing yourself to get stuck in your head, where your little nay-sayers, Moe and Schmoe, live. This is why, according to an article in the *New York Times* by Gia Kourlas, the acclaimed choreographer George Balanchine told his dancers, "'Don't think, dear, do.' . . . He wasn't telling dancers to turn off their brains; he was urging them to dance in the moment. It was meant to quell *overthinking*, as in, get out of your head . . . To dance fully without hesitation, without self-consciousness . . . It's *freedom*."[31]

Embrace imperfection. To just dive in, you must be willing to risk being messy and imperfect and potentially screwing up in the name of fully inhabiting and contributing to the situation at hand. I'd much rather see a speaker or performer mess up with great enthusiasm than endure a performance that is perfect to a fault. As the great composer Ludwig Von Beethoven (who apparently was noted for his ability to improvise) is quoted as saying, "To play a wrong note is insignificant; to play without passion is inexcusable!" Remember: What you're OK with, your audience will be OK with.

Practice Makes The Imperfect More Bearable

As with anything, the more you practice improvising, the easier it gets. And the results are well worth it. As my friend, Mary Lemmer, who runs a company called Improved that teaches improvisation techniques to executives, explains in her TED Talk, leaders and communicators who are skilled at improvisation are better able to ". . . adapt to change, build trust among teams, communicate clearly, and make decisions with limited information . . . Over time, practicing improv will help you handle anything that comes your way."[32]

Taking improv classes with people like Mary or the experts at the Second City improv company (or me, for that matter) is a great way to improve your ability to relax in the moment and trust yourself so you can let your Charismatic Presence fly.

Here are three ways to practice improv all by yourself:

- Pick an unfamiliar topic out of the blue (e.g., unicycling, butterfly catching, the origin of sandals) and speak on it aloud for five minutes as if you're the be-all and end-all expert.

- Hop onto Zoom, set a timer for three minutes, and record yourself giving a three-minute minilecture on a zany "how-to" topic (e.g., how to teach dogs to dance, how to climb mountains backward, how to sleep standing up).

- Pick three unrelated words (e.g., brick, turnip, sailboat) and improvise a two-minute story that uses all three words.

And please, don't stress when you practice. Push your inner judgers to the side and dare to have fun.

"Eleni, What Do I Do When I'm Asked a Question That Takes Me By Surprise?"

I can't tell you how many of my executive clients worry about managing a question out of left field that they either know little about or is completely outside their wheelhouse. Here's what I tell them:

How to answer when you *sort of* know the answer:

In this case, you want to be able to buy yourself some time. Here are a couple of responses that allow you to regroup for a moment and formulate on the spot:

- "What a great question. Give me a moment to think about it." (And then do just that. Take a sip of water. Practice F.B.I.—foot, breath, intention—to ground yourself, if it helps.)

- "Thank you for asking that question. Just to be sure I understood it, would you mind repeating it?"

Then, commit to answering the question as best you can. *Keep your answer simple and clear.* Stay close to the core of a single idea and explore it fully, much like master-level jazz musicians do when they improvise within a chord structure. To yet again quote jazz saxophone master Alexa Tarantino, "Develop one concrete goal and idea that makes sense to people."[33]

How to answer when you *absolutely don't know* the answer:

- "That's an excellent question. Unfortunately, I don't have a definitive answer for you. Let me go research it a bit, and I'll circle back to you with what I found out."

- "Great question. I have no idea how to answer that, but I wonder if someone in the audience does?" This not only takes the focus off you but also allows for the potential to make someone in the audience a rock star by sharing their knowledge.

- "That's a fantastic question and right up the alley of my colleague, George. George, would you like to take a shot at answering it?" (Note: Never do this unless you are sure your colleague really might know the answer.)

Like life, presentations and Q&A sessions are not always going to be smooth sailing. But if you're willing to embrace principle four and commit to going all-in with your intention, choices, and connection with your audience, you will be less inclined to be thrown by what comes at you in scripted or unscripted moments. You'll learn to *turn icky into sticky,* which builds your confidence, ups your Charismatic Presence, and makes for maximally magnetic presentations.

Presence Principle Four:
Commit Thyself

Commit To A Strong Intention. Before every presentation or spotlight moment, ask yourself, "What am I here to do in service to my audience of one or one thousand?" Write it down, and let it propel you.

Commit To Relentless Connection. Honor the sacred eight by choosing to connect (and keep connecting) with eyes and heart as fully as possible to the person (or people) you're speaking to.

Commit To Making Bold Choices. Make the strongest, clearest, stickiest choices you can make to help what you want to say be most impactful. And don't second-guess those choices.

Embrace Your Inner Improviser. Be willing to believe that you are a master improviser. Trust and follow Eleni's Rules of Improvisation and experiment with your willingness to leap into the murky middle of discomfort with both feet. You can always turn an "oops!" into an opportunity.

CHAPTER 7

Presence Principle Five:
Turn Thyself On

The most powerful weapon on earth is the human soul on fire.
FERDINAND FOCH

Priya, a young, budding entrepreneur, dropped by my office in a panic. She was on her way to give her business pitch to an audience of investors in hopes they would support her fledgling healthcare business. Struggling with an almost crippling case of shyness, and so soft-spoken that I had to lean forward to hear her, Priya quivered like a cornered deer.

"I don't know if I can do it," she said, "I'm so scared."

"Priya," I said, "what do you think your greater purpose is while you're here on this planet?"

She thought about it for a moment. "My purpose is to help others lead healthier lives."

"Does your new business help people do that?"

"Absolutely," she said.

"Then stand firmly in your deep purpose, in your 'soul role,' as a healer. Let it fuel you, and it will trump your fear and fire up your presentation."

Propelled by her soul role, Priya went resolutely to the presentation venue. Though she was shaking in her shoes, she spoke with an irresistible conviction. As a result, she not only felt less afraid, but she also attracted several potential investors, which ultimately helped her launch her company. Compelled by that same soul role, she went on to apply—and be accepted into—a prestigious PhD program. Now, with a doctorate in health administration, she's honoring her soul role as a healer on a greater playing field.

Priya is a shining example of the power and clarity that can occur for you as a speaker and communicator when you embrace the fifth presence principle: Turn Thyself On (So You Can Turn Other People On).

Mining The Power Of The Fifth Presence Principle

The fifth presence principle involves defining and embracing your soul role—your deepest purpose as a human being—and allowing it to fuel your presence and presentations. Your soul role is an even deeper purpose than the why, or intention, that fuels your presentation. And it transcends the circumstances or obstacles surrounding your presentation.

Nothing is more compelling than a person, a speaker, who is fully committed to fulfilling their soul role in the context of their presentation. As Ferdinand Foch, a French general and marshal of France, Great Britain, and Poland during the First World War, is quoted as saying, "The most powerful weapon on earth is the human soul on fire."

When I'm working with clients to pinpoint their soul role, I often ask them to first try to express it in a sentence, such as, "I'm here to help others reach their highest potential" (which, by the way, is my soul role). Then I suggest they distill the essence down into a slogan you could put on a T-shirt or on a bumper sticker (mine is "Be you! Aim high!") Finally, I have them distill the essence of the slogan into one defining word (mine is "Elevator").

My soul role snakes through everything I do, whether I'm giving a presentation skills training, working with an executive to increase their confident Charismatic Presence, or giving a keynote to a group of women in business. Whatever the delivery method (writing, coaching, teaching, speaking, singing) my soul role—being an "elevator," helping others reach their highest potential—is at its core.

This holds true for you and your soul role. Make no mistake, like Priya and me, you have a soul role that is yours alone. I like to think of it as metaphorically stamped on your little bottom at birth, a symbol of your marching orders while you trod the Earth.

Your soul role, your unique, passionate purpose, aligns with your unique talents and abilities. It's like a super intention, fueling you to move forward and take action. When you plug into your soul role, your Charismatic Presence goes into overdrive, ratcheting up your ability to be of lasting impact and influence. A speaker who is tapped into his soul role is enthusiastic, energized, and focused on making a real difference in the lives of his audience, even if he is giving a presentation on something as "mundane" as explaining the defining components of new computer software.

While the fifth presence principle is about allowing yourself to be lit from within by your soul role, it's also about playing to your strengths. This means harnessing the things you're good at and that you love (and prefer) to do to help yourself be as present and activated as possible. Because when you're turned on—physically and energetically—your audience will be, too. This includes knowing and embracing the performance styles (e.g., interactive trainings versus "sage from the stage" lecture-style presentations) that ratchet up your Charismatic Presence and awaken and engage your inner performer.

Invite Your Inner Performer To Come Out And Play

I like to imagine that each of us—even those of us who consider ourselves introverts or profess to hate public speaking—have an inner performer dying to come out and play. We just need to provide it with the right circumstances and materials.

You will put your inner performer (and potentially your audience) to sleep if you load up your presentation with material or activities you hate sharing or doing—like page after page of bullet points or numbers. You will make your inner performer pout in a corner and refuse to participate if you choose to dryly lecture your audience instead of engaging them in a sincere, conversational manner.

It's your duty as a speaker to excite, engage, and energize your inner performer. The more you do so, the more fun you'll have, and the more relaxed and present you'll be—and the more your audience can relax and enjoy the moment with you.

Even the least "theatrical" among us can customize a presentation that turns us (and our inner performer) on, suits our style, and engages our audience to the max.

Carol's Story: Go With What You Love To Do

Take Carol, a participant in one of my Think Like An Actor, Speak Like A Pro presentation skills public workshops. Smart, sweet, and extremely shy, Carol, an accountant, had spent the many years of her professional life happily crunching numbers. She had also spent the many years of her professional life being scared to death of giving public presentations.

When I asked her what, at the core, she was most passionate about in her life, Carol didn't hesitate: "I love helping people solve problems and understand things better." This passionate purpose was evident in the presentation topic that she chose: helping the audience members understand how and why their gross pay was reduced to a net dollar amount on their paychecks.

With a tiny, tremulous voice, Carol began to share her presentation. A minute into it, she did something I did not expect: She stepped off the stage and into the audience, clutching in her trembling hands what appeared to be a large wad of cash.

"These," she said, "are fake $1,000 bills. I'm going to give one to each of you. And I want you to pretend this is your paycheck." The more focused she became on walking around the room and handing the bills to each of us, the more her voice steadied, her inner performer came out to play, and her Charismatic Presence grew. At one point, she became downright bossy: "Hold up your money in both hands," she commanded. "Now, rip off a piece."

Utterly intrigued, we followed her prompt.

"That first piece goes to unemployment," she explained. "Now, rip off another piece!" As we ripped pieces off our fake money, Carol explained in detail what each piece represented. The audience was engaged from start to finish. And so was Carol.

When I think back to Carol's presentation, I realize that Carol had done two things right. The first was that she chose an interactive style—with a prop and related hands-on audience activities—which shifted the focus from her to the members of the audience. This took the pressure off her and allowed her to relax. The second thing she did—knowingly or unknowingly—was to hook her presentation up to her deepest, most passionate purpose, or soul role: Helping people understand things better, particularly with regard to money. By doing this, Carol's reason for delivering the presentation became more important than the self-defeating, fear-based voices of Moe and Schmoe, and she was able to leap boldly into her presentation.

Did the audience care that Carol was (at least initially) visibly nervous, with shaking hands? Nope. They were too busy following Carol's prompts and gleefully ripping up their fake money. When Carol was finished, they shared with great enthusiasm how much they appreciated her palpable passion for her topic and her commitment to making sure the audience understood what she was trying to convey.

The one-two punch of Carol choosing a presentation style that played to her strengths and hooked directly into her soul role made all the difference—for her and for her audience.

It takes thought, discipline, and time to determine what your soul role is, and what strengths, passions, and preferences float your boat as a speaker and turn on your inner performer. But they are key to honoring presence principle five because they keep the flame of your Charismatic Presence growing and glowing, no matter what.

Nobody is as invested as you are in realizing your soul role (which fuels your Charismatic Presence). The more you are willing to take responsibility to fan the flame of your soul role, the less you'll be thrown by the bumps and bruises you'll naturally encounter along your path to mastery as a speaker (like the one negative post-talk survey result in a sea of positive remarks or a single shaky performance that throw you for a loop).

I would be remiss if I didn't share with you one of the best ways I know to fan the flame of your soul role and thus maximize your Charismatic Presence: creating a vivid speaker vision—a detailed, compelling picture of how you want to feel, act, and be when you step into your next big spotlight moment.

Turn Yourself On (And Keep Yourself Turned On) With A Vivid Speaker Vision: See It On Paper, And In Your Head, Before You Experience It.

A speaker vision is a clearly delineated description of you successfully achieving your speaking or communicating goal. It's set in the future, on a specific date that you determine, but written in the present tense as if you are recording the moments as they unspool before you.

The idea is to fill your vision statement with such rich and specific details that when the day and event you've envisioned arrives, you can look around and think, "Hey, I recognize this. It's what I detailed in my vision statement."

Peak performers, like Olympian swimmer Michael Phelps, have long understood the power of envisioning an outcome in rich detail. By replaying the imaginary details of the preparation for an event, the event itself, and the immediate consequences of the event, they "live" the experience even if they haven't had it yet. When the day arrives for the actual event to play out, the details of the event feel comfortable and familiar, like a case of "been there, done that." The reason is the brain doesn't differentiate between living out something in your head and living it in real life. In essence, the experience you are imagining becomes real and a "done deal."

I'm a big believer that thoughts create beliefs, beliefs create habits, and habits become your reality (hence my focus on turning lies that bind into useful power phrases, as I laid out in chapter 3). Simply put, what you can imagine you can create. If you think about it, everything around you came into being because someone imagined it—from the chair you are seated on to the light fixture illuminating this page to the book in your hand (I can attest with absolute confidence to the truth of the latter).

A speaker vision statement (or, for that matter, a leadership vision or a personal vision statement) is incredibly powerful and empowering. It can act as both a magnet, drawing you toward it, or a driving force, pushing you forward, which is why I've been assigning it to my coaching clients for years.

Whether you're aiming to give a kickoff speech at your company's annual town hall meeting, perform at your peak in a job interview, or participate in a panel discussion, here are the steps to take to write a vivid speaker vision for that spotlight moment:

1. Grab a piece of paper and a pen (yes, I realize that's old-school analog, but writing with your hand on a piece of actual paper is a more direct line to your subconscious, from which the elements of this vision statement will flow).

2. At the top of the paper, write the date the spotlight moment will be occurring (or a date by which you want your vision statement to occur).

3. Now imagine the day—and your speaking engagement—unfolding, moment by moment. Write those details down in rich detail, as if it's occurring right now (e.g., "It's 7 a.m., and I've arrived early at the hotel ballroom to do a sound check for today's presentation"). Don't edit, just write. Remember to include the feelings you are experiencing as the day or talk unfolds (e.g., "Due to my thorough preparation, I feel as confident and ready as I could be"). Such feelings could include the added sense of confidence your preparation has given you, the excitement or pleasure at sharing your wisdom, your sense of ease and relaxation, your joy at connecting with your audience, and your pride in what you have accomplished.

Here are some details you might want to include:

- The steps you've taken up until that point to prepare for your spotlight moment.

- The way you feel and what R&R&R you engage in as you wait in the wings prior to stepping onto the stage or up to the microphone.

- Who is in the audience, and how they are reacting.

- How it feels to share your perspective and expertise with your audience.

- How you feel at the conclusion of your talk, as you receive kudos from your audience or colleagues.

You can find an example of a speaker vision statement (mine) in appendix B at the end of this book.

Once you write your vibrant vision statement, I strongly suggest you internalize it by doing the following:

- **Read it aloud** in the morning and the evening—or as often as you possibly can.

- **Record it on your phone.** Then listen to it right before you fall asleep and when you get up in the morning when your brain is at its most receptive.

- **Sit quietly once or twice a day and imagine the details** of the written vision statement as if you are watching the scenes in a video.

- **Read it to someone** who cares about you. There's something indescribably thrilling and empowering that occurs when you lay claim to your vision statement by speaking it aloud. The level of excitement and confidence you feel around the upcoming spotlight moment rises with each spoken word. I've seen this occur again and again when I ask participants in my Skygrabber Speaker Presentation Skills Deep Dive Workshop to stand up and share their written speaker vision statement. It's always goosebump time for both the person reading it and those of us listening.

The more you embrace your speaker vision statement, the more it will imprint itself in your subconscious and add to your inner sense of confidence, boosting your Charismatic Presence. This can have a huge, positive impact on your performance the day the spotlight moment you've described on paper rolls around. As a coaching client said to me after giving a winning, career-defining sales presentation for which she'd written and internalized a powerful vision statement, "It felt like I'd been there before. The details of what I experienced felt so familiar—and now I was just living them moment by moment like I had in my head for weeks."

You Are The Keeper Of The Flame

No one can write and internalize your vivid vision, define and honor your soul role, or acknowledge and maximize your unique strengths except you. You are the keeper of the flame that is at the core of your Charismatic Presence.

So, what about you? What might your soul role be? What are you here to do at the deepest level? What's the passionate purpose that fuels you? What one word does it boil down to (like "teacher," "catalyst," or "healer")? Your soul role is a mighty force, and it's your responsibility to stay connected to it and to keep its flames fanned. Are you willing to connect to it and let it fuel you before your next presentation?

And, stylistically speaking, what type of presentations do you prefer to give? Ones that rely heavily on slides, or ones with few or none? Workshops where you wander through your audience and encourage interactivity or lectures where you share your wisdom from the stage? Virtual via Zoom presentations or live in-person talks? How might you find a way to bring those stylistic elements into whatever presentation you are asked to deliver, like choosing to step off the stage to make a keynote more interactive?

And what are you good at, that you love to do, that you could enthusiastically include in your presentations? I know speakers who turn themselves and their audiences on by including poems or songs they've written (I do the latter), who juggle (knives, machetes, and power saws—

this speaker was once a Cirque du Soleil performer), who share relevant, fascinating quotes from their favorite books, who tell funny or moving personal stories to make their points more sticky (I'm one of those speakers) or who use silly, unforgettable props (like my Speaker Hall of Fame pal, Tim Gard. His use of signature props, including a rubber chicken whose feet stick out of his carry-on bag when he travels, makes you both laugh out loud and more deeply ingest his point.) What might you include that could turn on your inner performer and potentially invigorate dry-as-toast material so you can enliven both yourself and your audience?

Finally, are you willing to try writing a vivid speaker vision as another way to fire up your soul role and goose your Charismatic Presence?

I hope so. As a speaker, it is ultimately your responsibility to turn yourself on, which, in turn, turns your audience on. By committing to presence principle five, you ensure your audience of one or many will see and hear a human being who is alive, present, and imbued with passionate purpose—and who is having fun, to boot.

Knowing and embracing all five of the presence principles can help you up your game as a speaker and take your Charismatic Presence to new levels of magnetism. Once you've done so, it's time to consider what comes next: maintenance and mastery.

Presence Principle Five:
Turn Thyself On

What's Your Soul Role? Looking back at your life and work, what is the underlying theme that snakes through? Could you narrow it down to one word, like "teacher," "fixer," or "catalyst"? What might a T-shirt or bumper sticker slogan say that represents the essence of your soul role? Write it down.

Write A Speaker Vision Statement. Remember to write the date the speaking engagement will be occurring at the top of the page. Write it as if the day/event is unspooling in front of you, in the present moment. Include vivid details and emotions. Then, read it, listen to it, and internalize it.

Determine Your Preferred Speaking Style. The more you identify your preferred way of delivering presentations (e.g., formal lecture, interactive workshop, virtual versus live in-person), the more you can play to your strengths.

What Turns You On? Make a list of the things you like to do or do well, like juggling, singing, or telling stories. How might you be able to include these talents and activities in your presentations?

PART III

After You Have Upped Your Game

CHAPTER 8

Moving Toward Mastery: Ten Ways To Sustain Presence And Presentation Excellence

The road to mastery requires patience.
You will have to keep your focus on five or ten years down the road
when you will reap the rewards of your efforts.
ROBERT GREENE

Once you've turned up the heat on your Charismatic Presence and upped your game as a presenter, it's your responsibility to keep it up. This means not only doing what it takes to maintain a consistent level of excellence but continuously reaching toward higher levels of proficiency.

Keeping the flame of your Charismatic Presence lit and your skillsets as a presenter growing is essentially a lifelong endeavor. Peak performers of all kinds commit to developing mastery in their chosen disciplines over the course of their lives. Fueled by their soul role, they understand the value of pushing themselves to move toward the next level of artistry and are willing to step again and again into the murky middle of discomfort between what they know and what they don't know yet.

It pays to think like an actor and commit to presence and presentation mastery by engaging in regular activities designed to keep you centered, fired up, and progressing as a speaker and communicator. Here are ten practices that can help you do just that.

1. Ask yourself *the four questions*. After every spotlight moment you engaged in, ask yourself the following: Did I solve my intention? What went better than expected? What didn't go as well as I'd hoped? What could I do differently the next time? Then, honor the answer to the final question by taking a different action or approach for your next presentation.

2. Commit to caring for your voice, body, and head, the tools you rely on as a speaker. This means regularly doing exercises to warm up and strengthen your body (yoga, strength training, walking—whatever gets you moving) and your voice (do tongue twisters, hum your favorite tunes, take voice lessons, refrain from yelling and potentially hurting your vocal cords, use a microphone when you're speaking to more than thirty people for over thirty minutes). Be vigilant about your mental health: Get a good therapist if you need help managing anxiety or stress; meditate or do mindful breathing regularly; write your wrongs out in a journal.

3. Take an improvisation class and learn how to dance with your butterflies. Look for local branches of the Second City or the Groundlings, two powerhouse improvisation groups that have spawned comedy greats like Tina Fey, Stephen Colbert, Will Ferrell, and Kristen Wiig. Check out my pal Mary Lemmer's excellent improvisation for business programming at https://www.chooseimprove.com/.

4. Say "yes" to as many speaking opportunities as possible. The more you speak, the better you get.

5. Push yourself to go the next level and try something a little scary—like standing up and presenting if you're used to sitting when you give a talk, speaking in front of a larger audience than you're accustomed to, or volunteering to be first or last in a lineup of speakers (if neither is something you'd prefer to do).

6. Work with a coach to help you create and rehearse presentations and help you minimize any habits and behaviors that are keeping you from performing at your peak.

7. Learn to speak extemporaneously (from brief notes) rather than being stuck to a script. To do this, once you've created a presentation script (if that is your tendency), immediately create a skeleton outline with clumps of keywords and bullet points based on your script. Practice the presentation aloud using the outline, only referring to the script when you absolutely need to. Then, make another even more skeletal version of the outline. Practice it aloud until the gist of what you want to say is consistent but not word-for-word. And yes, you can use your outline when you talk, so long as your eyes aren't glued to it.

8. Watch and learn from master-level speakers. Go to TED.com to watch some super-duper thought leaders brilliantly share their big ideas (Dr. Brené Brown's talk on courage and vulnerability is a must). Take note of their physical relaxation, relatability, and clarity.

9. Videotape and watch your presentations, both when you're giving them to an audience and when you're rehearsing them (easy to do on Zoom or other such virtual platforms). Yes, I know it's painful, but it's the only way you'll see, hear, and learn what tics and habits might be getting in the way of your efforts as a speaker, as well as what is working and flowing well.

10. Engage in **Daily F.B.I. practice.** By this I mean use an extended version of the foot—breath—intention preshow or recovery tool I shared with you in chapter 5 to fire up your Charismatic Presence and ground yourself before you start your day or begin a presentation rehearsal.

   ○ **F is for "Foundation."** Standing with your feet shoulder length apart, grounding yourself by feeling the floor with the soles of your feet. Then, *fill your space* by standing in a power pose, either with your hands at your waist like Superman or in a V for victory above your head. *Feed your purpose* by taking a moment to connect with your soul role, the deepest "why" that drives you. If you can recall and recite your personal manifesto (or listen to it via headphones), do it.

   ○ **B is for "Breathe" and "Be."** Engage in mindful belly breathing (ten breaths in and out, with a count of four on the inhalation, hold on two, exhale on six). Then, wake up your voice by blowing air through pursed lips, like a baby blowing spit bubbles, and making up and down sounds, like an emergency siren, using the word "bee."

   ○ **I is for "Intention."** Remember the task at hand and what you are there to do at a core level in relation to your day or your work on your presence or presentation. *Invoke* a useful power phrase, like "I am here" or "I am relaxed and ready," or support from a higher power (e.g., "I ask for guidance and support in staying true to my deepest intention and being of greatest value as a speaker and communicator").

Use the graphic below as a guide.

F. B. I.
DAILY PRESENCE PRACTICE

3.
I = INTENTION
Invocation/Power Phrase
Focus on Task at Hand

2.
B = BREATHE & BE
Belly Breathing & Relaxation
Vocal Warm Up
("B-b-b-b "& "Beeeeeee")

1.
F = FOUNDATION
Find Footing
Fill Space
Feed Purpose
(Personal Manifesto; Soul Role)

The more you commit to practices that encourage presence and presentation mastery, the more confident and engaging you will be as a communicator and speaker, and the more your Charismatic Presence will grow and strengthen over time.

Moving Toward Mastery

Pick A Practice. Which of the ten mastery practices would you be willing to commit to embracing first? Second? Third? Choose practices that bolster an area that you know needs support and development and implement them regularly.

Keep A Post-Presentation Notebook. In a dedicated paper notebook or in a folder on a digital device, record your responses to The Four Questions after every important spotlight moment (presentation, meeting, etc.). What trends do you notice? Make adjustments accordingly going forward.

Check In With Reliable Sources. Who are your trusted sources for presence and presentation critique? A coach? A mentor? Regularly ask them to give you targeted input on your progress to keep you moving forward toward mastery.

CHAPTER 9

Three Presentation Patterns To Build Your Talks

There's freedom in the form.
ANNE BOGART

I come from a line of women who sew. Vasiliki Plakias, my maternal grandmother—or Yiayia, in Greek—was an entrepreneurial seamstress who sewed gorgeous, high-end lingerie out of lace and satin for wealthy ladies.

My mother, Theresa, told me that when she was a little girl, she would sit at my Yiayia's feet and pick up the pins that dropped onto the floor. And from that vantage point, literally at my Yiayia's knee, she learned how to sew. From as far back as I can remember, Ma sewed all her own clothes—and mine, too. Pants, dresses, skirts, blouses, you name it, she could sew it.

I loved sitting with Ma and watching her sew. It was downright magical to see how pieces of fabric could come together to make a beautiful skirt or dress. It was also instructional, as I quickly learned the basic elements of sewing by observation and a little bit of hands-on practice.

Soon, I was making my own clothes, which always started with buying a sewing pattern representing the finished outfit I intended to make. A sewing pattern, in case you're wondering, is a paper template of the parts of a piece of clothing that you trace or pin onto fabric before you cut them out and sew them together in a specific order. You can use the same pattern again and again, customizing it for different occasions by changing up components like the length or the material you make it from.

In Praise Of Presentation Patterns

Using patterns for sewing is one of the reasons I like patterns in general—they are underlying structures and systems that help put something in place. I like a *there*, there. It's why I wished I had a pattern to follow when I had to create my first professional talk for a prestigious conference years ago. While I had an idea of what I wanted the talk to look and feel like, I didn't have the faintest idea of how to construct it (which holds true for most of the coaching clients I work with). After a little bit of procrastination, I fired up my computer and started noodling away. And the more I noodled, the more confused I got.

I wondered, "How do I start? What comes next? What comes after that? What do I keep in? What do I leave out?" And then it got so overwhelming that I started flinging a bunch of ideas at my computer screen and hoped to God that they would somehow miraculously come together.

That's what it was like for me for a long time. Until one day I thought, "What if I put together a pattern based on talks I've seen that I really liked."

And so that's what I did. First, I created a pattern for a long-form, keynote-length presentation. And it worked like gangbusters. And that keynote pattern gave me an idea of how to create a pattern for a short talk. And out of that short talk pattern came a pattern for a teeny tiny talk.

I started using these patterns myself and teaching them to my clients. They loved them, and no wonder—they provided order, focus, and clarity for both my clients and their audience.

Look at it like this: You wouldn't try to cook a complicated dish without a recipe to follow. You wouldn't try to build a house without a blueprint. So why would you try to create a presentation without an underlying structure or system to nudge the parts of your presentation into place? And why not have a blueprint that you can use time and again to create and customize other presentations down the road so you don't have to reinvent the wheel every time?

A great presentation starts with a great pattern. With that in mind, here are three presentation patterns that I've created and rely on, that you can use for all manner of talks, forever.

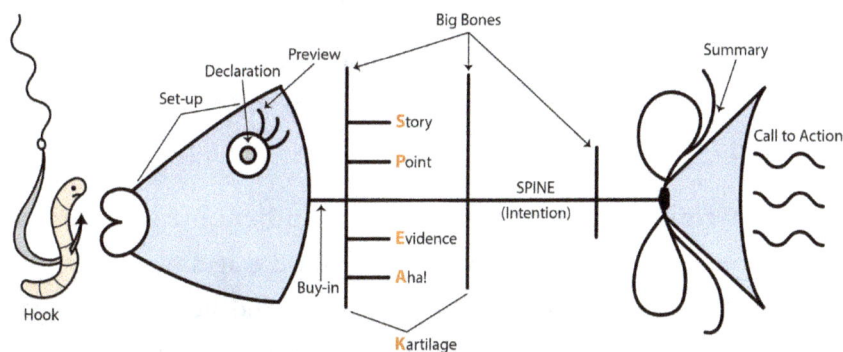

Presentation Pattern One: Eleni's Fabulous Fishbone Formula (Or EFFF)

Best for presentations from ten to sixty minutes long, this is the big daddy of my presentation blueprints. I've had clients swoon over it because it makes putting together and remembering a long-form presentation (like a keynote or even a workshop or training) so much easier to do. It's modular, meaning it's in various parts that you can expand out or contract in depending on the length of your talk, and it is customizable to your specific audience and its needs.

There are three parts to the fishbone: the head, the tail, and everything in between (what I call the body). Each one of those parts is like a mini presentation, with a beginning, middle, and end all its own. Before I explain each of the three components, I want to point out what holds them all together: the spine of the fish or the presentation intention, which is by far the most important part of your presentation.

The Intention

Your intention is the overarching *why*, purpose, or *theme* of the talk, which I wrote about at length in chapter 5. It's what you're there to do in service to your audience. The stronger the intention/spine, the less floppy the presentation/fish. Your intention is the skewer that holds the whole presentation together and keeps you from going off into the weeds.

To determine your intention, you need to *position your presentation*. This means tailoring it to the unique audience you are serving. Here's how you do that:

- **Determine the composition of the audience** (e.g., first-time entrepreneurs, mixed genders, between the ages of twenty-four to forty-nine, in the greater Detroit area, who are on the verge of sharing a business pitch at a local pitch competition).

- **Determine the pain/problem/challenges** they are facing that you are uniquely there to solve (e.g., These first-time entrepreneurs have rarely, if ever, given a business pitch. They don't know how to craft one, much less how to deliver it under pressure. And they're nervous and scared).

- **Determine why you are the perfect fit** as a speaker. What gives you the right to share your wisdom with this group? (e.g., I've spent the better part of twenty years helping entrepreneurs craft and deliver moneymaking pitches. And I've been the go-to presentation skills coach and trainer for three Detroit-area entrepreneurial incubators.) This is where your commonality with your audience, your confidence, and the stories you can use within your presentation come from.

Once you've made those determinations, you're ready to craft your intention statement. Here's a simple formula to use:

My intention is to _____ so you can _____.

It's a two-part formula: The first part is what you're there to do as a speaker. The second part is what the audience needs and wants.

I gave you some examples of intentions in chapter 6.

BODY OF THE FISH

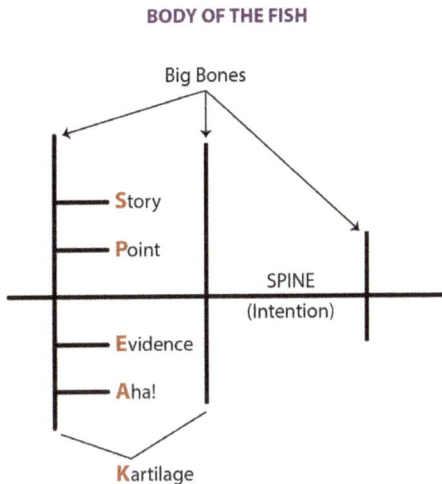

Big Bones

Story

Point

SPINE
(Intention)

Evidence

Aha!

Kartilage

Now, let's look at the body of the fish.

Body Of The Fish

Think of the body of the fish representing the chapters of an instructional or self-help book that come after the introduction chapter and before the final closing chapter. In the case of my fishbone, the "chapters" of the body of the fish are what I call the big bones. They are the three to five main topics or ideas you've chosen to support the overall intention. I say three to five because your audience can't really handle more than that amount of information. Here's how I like to structure each big bone, using what I call my **S.P.E.A.K.** technique:

S is for "Story." Start with a story that sets up or illustrates the point that is at the core of the big bone. Personal stories or client mess-to-success stories (that show how you moved them from frustration or confusion to clarity and empowerment) are best. Why stories? Because stories are sticky. They are easy for you and your audience to remember and can make your point come alive.

Show, don't tell, the story—meaning, bring it to life with rich, active details the way you would if you were telling it around the dinner table or to a friend while having a cocktail. Speak for characters in the story (e.g., "So Grandma said, 'take your dirty feet off my coffee table, young man.'" versus "Grandma told me to take my feet off the coffee table.").

If you can't come up with an appropriate story, find an analogy or use a series of questions to set the stage for the point you're poised to make.

P is for "Point." Explain in one clear and memorable sentence what the point is of the story you just told. If you can boil it down into a simple sticky phrase that can act as an audience takeaway (e.g., "When you shrink to fit, you take a hit"), so much the better.

E is for "Evidence." Now shore up and unpack the point by providing further elaboration in the form of data, examples, visuals, quotes—whatever you think might help drive your point home. Think of this section as scaffolding that serves to reinforce your point.

A is for "Aha!/Application." Ask a hypothetical question designed to get the audience to think about the point you've made as it relates to them. I call this a "turnaround" or "What about you?" moment. The more you can help the members of the audience relate to your point, the more they will retain it.

Here's an example: "Think about that for a minute: How much more productive and stress-free do you think you might be if you were willing to try using my fabulous fishbone formula when you put a presentation together?"

Suppose you are putting together a training or workshop where the focus is on your audience doing most of the work rather than on you. In that case, this is the section you can expand out to include more experiential learning activities like individual writing exercises, small group conversations about a topic, paired practice, etc.

K is for "Kartilage" *(misspelled, I know)*. The "kartilage" is the connective tissue between two big bones. This critical juncture between the wrapping up of one idea and the introduction of another is often where speakers stumble because they haven't thought it through.

To create a smooth and memorable transition, reinforce your point once again, and then tip your audience into the next bone by hinting about what's coming next (without giving away the whole premise): "Now you know the value of doing the work to be fully present when you speak and communicate. But what does it take to manage the limiting beliefs that can make you second-guess yourself before you step into the spotlight?"

Think like a professional actor who would never step into a scene on stage without knowing where she is coming from as a character and why she is stepping into the scene.

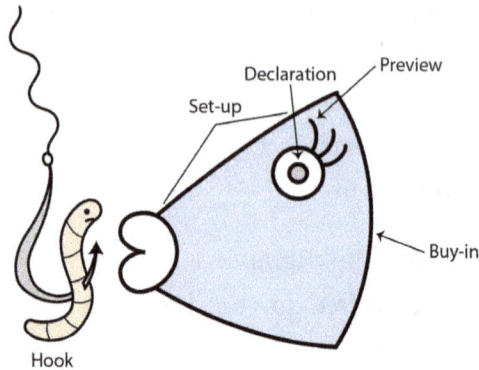

Head Of The Fish

This is the most important part of your presentation, second only to the intention statement. Unfortunately, it also tends to be one of the weakest.

Do you see the white space right before the tail of the unfortunate worm on the fishbone graph? I call that the magic moment, the moment of anticipation right before the speaker opens their mouth and breaks the silence for the first time.

In that moment, the audience is thinking, "What's she going to sound like? Is she going to hold my attention?"

It doesn't take much to blow the magic moment. Just start by saying the same things the audience has already heard too many times, like "Hi everyone. How's it going this morning? So, my name is _____, and I'm going to give a presentation on _____" (which the audience already knows, since you have already been introduced and the title of the talk is on the screen behind them). Talk about wishy-washy.

You have less than seven seconds to make an impression on your audience, good or bad.[34] Make your first words count. Break the silence with a great hook.

Hook: The hook is the first thing out of your lips that officially kicks off your presentation (as opposed to, say, a brief thank you or quip made to your host before you take a breath and start your speech). It should make people sit up, scooch their butts forward on their seats, and get their eyebrows to raise.

My favorite hooks are:

- A story that sets up the premise/pain/problem you're there to solve. Particularly effective is a story that illustrates something the audience doesn't want (the challenges they're facing) or, conversely, one that illustrates something the audience longs for (how they might feel if their challenges were solved).

- A question or series of questions—hypothetical or one that demands audience response—that opens the door to what you're there to solve. (e.g., "How many of you would rather leap into a tub of live rats than speak in public? Raise your hand.")

- A startling statement that does the same. (e.g., "Eighty. That's the percentage of people who feel 'meh' about speaking in public. Eighty percent. That's a lot of 'meh' presentations.")

The hook should metaphorically pull the audience through the door (the fish's lips) and into the next part of the fish's head.

Set-up (of the problem): Once you've hooked your audience, help them know you know what they are struggling with by spelling out the pain and problems on a high level: "Too many speakers worry too much about being perfect, impressing others, looking bad, and messing up. To make matters worse, they often don't know how to organize and deliver a presentation, which adds to their stress and fear. And speaking of fear, most people have no idea how to manage the fight-or-flight fear-based adrenaline rush that can ambush them right before they step into the spotlight. And the more they capitulate to the fear, the more their natural Charismatic Presence diminishes, and the less impact they have as speakers and leaders."

Declaration of intention: Once you've highlighted the issues and challenges you're there to solve, let your audience know what you're there to do by sharing your intention statement: "I don't want fear to stop you from sharing your wisdom when it matters. That's why I'm here: My intention is to convince you to think like an actor so that you can be more relaxed, present, and effective when you pitch or present."

Preview (of coming attractions): Following your declaration of intention, let your audience know where you're going to take them on their journey with you. Essentially, you're highlighting (without much or any detail) the essence of the big bones you're going to talk about with them. The preview is the equivalent of what you might think of as the agenda (although I generally dislike agenda slides). Too many speakers start their presentations at the preview/agenda and miss out on the incredible opportunity to connect with their audience that including a strong hook, set up, and declaration of intention can provide.

Buy-in: Finish out the head of the fish with a little moment of connection with your audience that elicits their buy-in going forward: "By the time I'm done, I'm hoping you'll not only have a more positive perspective on giving presentations, but useful tools to help you elevate your public speaking abilities. Does that sound good? Let's dive in."

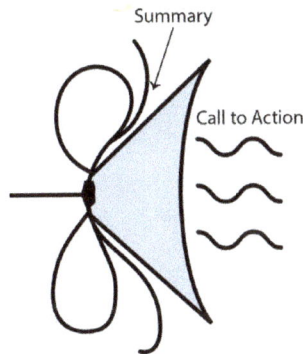

Tail Of The Fish

How many times have I witnessed a speaker end their presentation by saying something like, "Oh my gosh, I'm out of time. Does anybody have any questions?"

Yes, I have a question: *Why are you ending in such a wishy-washy fashion?* The tail of the fish is a critical part of your presentation, so don't toss it off. Tie your presentation together for a strong finish.

There are two parts to the tail of the fish:

Summary: Symbolized by the bow in the fishbone graphic, your summary helps your audience remember what you want them to remember. To do this, reiterate the takeaways of the big bones (which your audience has no doubt already forgotten).

FYI, the knot in the bow is a reminder that, by this point in the presentation, you've earned the trust of your audience as well as the right to ask them to engage in a collective, dramatic action that reinforces the overall message. For example, you could have everyone raise their right hand and swear an oath, write down a task they're committed to completing, or stand up and sing a chorus of a song together (something I do with my Touch The Sky keynote audience).

Call to action: Research shows that people remember the last thing you said (it's called the proximity effect), so make the final words of your talk count.

End definitively with a strong call to action—something you want your audience to think about or do as a result of what you've shared with them (e.g., "I challenge you to say yes to every opportunity to step up in front of a group and share your wisdom. Because your words and perspective matter. Use your words to change your world. Thank you.").

The end of your presentation should feel like the end, so make sure to drop your voice when you speak your final words. It should be the speaking equivalent of the "And that is that" moment when a basketball player dunks the ball dramatically and definitively through the net.

When you use my fishbone blueprint, I suggest you approach it in this order:

1. Position your presentation and create a compelling intention statement.

2. Define the three to five big bones and the takeaway point of each bone.

3. Craft the content (S.P.E.A.K.) of the big bones.

4. Flesh out the head of the fish.

5. Flesh out the tail of the fish.

Presentation Pattern Two: Short Talk Technique (S.P.E.A.K.)

My short talk blueprint came right out of my fabulous fishbone formula when I realized that the method I was using for arranging a big bone could be used to put together a rockin' short talk. When you've got to create and deliver a five-to-seven-minute talk, this is a great way to go.

S is for "Story." Start with a story that illustrates the central pain/problem/challenge you're there to solve. In a sense, the story in this short talk pattern serves as the hook, the setup, and the declaration, driving to the overall point.

P is for "Point." Explain in one clear and memorable sentence what the point of the story is that you just told.

E is for "Evidence." Now, unpack the point a little bit by providing further elaboration in the form of data, examples, etc.

A is for "Aha!/Application." Ask a hypothetical question designed to get the audience to think about the point you've made as it relates to them.

K is for "Konclusion" *(yep, misspelled again)*. Bring your rockin' short talk to a close by reminding your audience of your overarching point and ending with a call to action (something you want them to think about or do).

Presentation Speaking Pattern Three: Teeny Tiny Talk Blueprint (TPTP)

This is a simple method for putting together a minuscule talk (one to three minutes long). It's also a really great blueprint for brief marketing/social media videos.

T is for "Tale." Set up your premise with a story.

P is for "Point." Make the *point* of the story.

T is for "Turnaround." Flip the perspective to that of the audience. This is the same sort of "What about you?" moment in the S.P.E.A.K. technique designed to help the audience think about the point you've made as it relates to them.

P is for "Period." Bring your teeny, tiny talk to a close by repeating your point and ending with a call to action.

Now, you know three useful, customizable presentation patterns or blueprints. Will you try using them? Or are you perhaps thinking, "I don't want to use a structure, or pattern, or blueprint, or whatever you want to call it? It's too restrictive, it's too formulaic."

There's Freedom In The Form

Here's what I have to say to you if you're worried that presentation patterns will somehow handcuff you:

A pattern or structure isn't meant to bind you. It's meant to free you up, by giving you an organized, safe space to play and create. It's like a playpen for a kid or a roped-off swimming area at the beach that the lifeguard can survey.

Simply put, **structure creates safety and freedom.** As my favorite theater director, Anne Bogart, once said to me, "There's freedom in the form." Just as a playpen allows a child to play safely, the boundaries of a blueprint give you the freedom to surrender to the moment and unleash your Charismatic Presence.

Structure also makes the process simpler and less stressful by taking away the guesswork of laying out a presentation. It helps you know what goes where and when. It also enables you to know what to leave in and, most importantly, what to leave out. That's especially helpful with short talks where every second and every word counts.

Finally, patterns and structures help you remember your talk. That's because they typically have a narrative flow and a clear beginning, middle, and end. They're telling a story, and your brain loves and remembers stories. This is a big plus when nerves and adrenaline kick in.

Consider trying one or all the presentation blueprints I've shared and see how they might positively affect the way you design and deliver your next presentations. The more you use these presentation patterns, the more familiar they'll become to you and the more masterful you'll be at designing your presentation.

One final note: Even with a presentation pattern in hand, you might need help from an outside source to guide you through the process. Several top-level speaker clients have come back to me, again and again, to help them hammer together their signature talks. The fact that we share a common vocabulary (e.g., hook, big bone, declaration of intention, etc.) helps the process go faster. It's all about maintaining consistency and moving toward mastery in your presence and presentations.

Three Presentation Blueprints To Build Your Talk

First And Foremost, Position Your Presentation. No matter what presentation pattern you choose, start by determining the makeup of the audience, their unique pain/problems/challenges, your fit in relation to those challenges, and a strong and driving intention statement. This will ensure you give a customized talk with a strong, guiding purpose/big idea.

Play With A Pattern. Knowing the Fishbone is best for longer form talks, and the SPEAK and TPTP patterns are best for shorter talks, take the risk to play with using one for your next talk. Experiment with the patterns and determine which you find most useful.

Structure First, Content Second. When you create a presentation, stop yourself from starting by designing slides and determining content. Instead, first, build the structure using the blueprints, then add the flesh (content). Remember that slides are not structural; they are content choices.

One Story, One Point. When using a story to illustrate your point/takeaway, don't confuse your audience by using the story to make multiple points. Keep it simple.

CHAPTER 10

Into The Future

By changing nothing, nothing changes.
Tony Robbins

I was waiting in the wings, poised to step out onto the stage to deliver a keynote at a conference, when my host turned to me and said, "Eleni, guess what! You're going to have walk-on music!"

"Really?" I said, surprised. "What kind of music?" As a singer and songwriter, I admit I'm picky about any music that's associated with me.

"It's an original song," she replied, "generated by artificial intelligence—AI. My pal, Tim McNeely, fed the theme of your talk and some phrases from your website into ChatGPT, which created lyrics. Then he plugged those lyrics into an AI-based song generator that's called Suno, with the suggestion that the feel and melody be like a Broadway show tune, and that's how your song was born."

And right then, a peppy song started blasting through the loudspeakers. Sure enough, I recognized some of the words and phrases that are part of my brand: "presence," "truth," "lead with power." As I stepped onto the stage, joining my host in dancing along to the beat of the song, I had two thoughts in quick succession:

1. "Holy _____! That is so ridiculously cool. AI is *amazing*." (That was the tech nerd in me talking.)

2. "Holy _____! This AI songwriting thing could put professional songwriters out of business unless they make friends with the technology." (That was the singer-songwriter in me talking.)

In a nutshell, I was both thrilled and horrified by the ability of AI to do something that previously only humans had been able to do: write songs with lyrics. And frankly, whatever opinion I might have had of the song as a song was insignificant in the face of its rather miraculous birth.

Generative AI tools, like the kind that Tim McNeely used to generate my song, let users enter prompts in return for AI-created humanlike text, images, and videos. Much like the telephone or the internet, these AI-based tools have upended the way we create and disseminate information. They're only one of the plethora of technologies and tools available to humans in general and speakers in particular in this tech-focused day and age.

Like any major disruption, these new technologies (virtual platforms, content-producing AI systems, and apps that support the creation and delivery of presentations, etc.) have both advantages and disadvantages for speakers who want to develop and share their message with a maximum of Charismatic Presence. And they are well worth exploring and embracing.

In addition to these game-changing tech tools and trends, there is a trend toward pared-down simplicity and brevity in presentations and toward an emphasis on visual components like images and video.

Let's look at some of these technologies and trends, starting with the one that altered our behavior entirely when we were broadsided by a deadly virus that took the world by surprise.

Virtual Presentations: The New Norm

When the COVID-19 pandemic hit in March 2020, I was instantly thrust into a strange, virtual world like everyone on the planet. Hunkered down in my home office, facing my computer screen, I knew I had to pivot to a 100 percent online speaking, training, and coaching model, or my business would die. It was a sobering moment during a dark time.

Fortunately, I was familiar with Zoom and Skype, having been using those platforms for several years to coach nonlocal, national, and international clients. What I was less familiar with was giving keynotes or large-scale training to groups via an online platform that reduced me to a thumbnail on a screen and threatened to lessen the impact of my Charismatic Presence. My presentation skills clients shared the very same issues and worries: "How do I manage the virtual technology so that it doesn't throw me? How do I make my presentations engaging if I can't see or hear my clients? How do I not become overly self-conscious when I see myself on screen?"

As a presentation expert, I understood that I had to quickly master speaking on virtual platforms so that I could help my clients do the same. The learning curve was, at times, brutal. But it served as a great reminder that change will always come, and if you want to continue to be relevant as a speaker and leader, you've got to ride the crest of the wave of change so you don't get swamped by it. Simply put (and this hearkens back to one of the rules of improvisation I shared in chapter 3), you've got to rock and roll with what you're given.

For better or worse, I leaped onto the virtual bandwagon, and so did my clients.

During the heat of the pandemic, I delivered online (and sometimes hybrid virtual plus live in-person while wearing a mask) training and keynote presentations. So did my clients. We learned (by trial and error) that we needed to amp up our preparation and preshow R&R&R relaxation techniques and master the tech (and/or have someone tech-savvy help us produce our presentations) so we could focus on delivering our message and connecting with the audience.

We learned camera technique 101: Look straight into the camera and talk to it like it's our best friend (or, as actors are taught, "Make love to the camera") so that every member of our online audience feels we're talking to them alone.

We learned (with great relief) that many of the engagement techniques we liked to do live in person also worked well in a virtual setting—like pairing people up, but in virtual breakout rooms—and that whatever didn't work could be replaced with another creative solution. By flinging our arms wide to the virtual experience, we learned we could be surprisingly innovative with online engagement tools.

That said, we also learned that nothing truly replaces the connection that happens when we're in a room together, breathing the same air, feeling each other's energies, and looking into each other's eyes.

Nonetheless, speaking and communicating on virtual platforms is here to stay. Why? Event planners and corporate entities have learned that hosting live online events can save a lot of money. Speakers and consultants learned that they don't need to leave the comforts of their home to share their message and be of value to perhaps an even larger number of people spread out over an even larger geographic area.

The acceptance of online conferences and speaking opportunities means that the virtual communication and presentation tools we learned during the height of the pandemic will not go to waste and will continuously need to be refined. It also means that the anxiety that comes from being spotlighted, warts and all, in a rectangular virtual thumbnail video for all to see (what I call Zoom performance anxiety or ZPA) will continue to be an issue to overcome for many presenters and communicators.

That said, at this writing, 95 percent of my post-pandemic presentations are being delivered live in person. While at first, it felt odd and a bit clunky to step in front of people again in real-time ("Where's the Zoom chat function and the hand-raising option? Where are all the notes I taped to my computer screen?"), it was, for me, a relief.

I love speaking to people in the flesh. This is not so for many of my clients; however, as I have discovered in the surveys I provide to my training audiences, I'd say that roughly 75 percent of the people I've surveyed feel measurably less anxious presenting on a virtual platform than they do while presenting in person. They like the separation the screen gives them and the feeling of control provided by being in their own environment ("command central," I call it).

The danger here lies in letting that separation from the audience (compounded by the ability of audience members to mute themselves and turn off their video feed) inhibit the speaker's ability to genuinely connect with the folks on the other side of the screen. Because even the most awesome technology, when used without care and intention, can minimize your Charismatic Presence.

Advancements in technology are, of course, part and parcel of our development as a species. And the thing about technology is that it's fun and exciting! We humans love playing with toys at any age, especially new ones.

Let's take a deeper look into one of the more compelling (and controversial) tech "toys" out there: AI-driven content generators like ChatGPT.

Let's Chitchat About ChatGPT

I was recently working with a coaching client, teasing out the content of a high-level keynote. As we noodled around with the phraseology for a particular section of her speech, she paused for a minute and tapped on her computer keys.

"What do you think about this?" she asked, sharing a particularly well-turned phrase that summarized the point we'd been brainstorming around.

"Dang!" I said, "That's really good."

"Yeah, well, that phrase is courtesy of ChatGPT. I just put in some keywords, and it coughed up that awesome content." I was, to put it mildly, floored.

In my experience, when it comes to presentations, AI content-generating tools, like ChatGPT or Claude, can help you do a few things quite well: flesh out ideas and phrases, determine catchy presentation titles, structure the outline of a presentation, and write a marketing description of the presentation you've put together. They can even write a complete speech based on a brief outline.

As Tim McNeely, the man responsible for the presentation walk-on song I wrote about at the top of this chapter, said to me, "AI is a tool that lets me brainstorm with myself. It's great for rapid prototyping."

Tim also said, "There's still something about the human experience that AI can never capture." I tend to agree with Tim that AI-developed speech content lacks (at least for now) the depth and breadth of humor, personality, emotion, and unique sensibilities that a real-life human might bring to it. AI doesn't replace the ineffable qualities of authenticity and the human factor.

AI can, however, certainly help you write a speech that you can then edit and augment with your signature stories, warmth, and perspective. And, of course, all the AI and tech in the world will not take the place of the work you need to do to practice and finesse the delivery of your presentation so you can be fully present with optimal Charismatic Presence flowing.

And Speaking Of Delivery . . . !

That said, there do exist technology-based tools that can help you improve your public speaking skills and delivery.[35] For instance, Speechace can evaluate such things as pace, pitch, and pronunciation. And Orai can, among other things, point out your filler words ("uhm," "eh," "like," "you know").

Zoom now has a feature, "enable smart recording with AI companion," which has a "meeting coach" option that gives you metrics around your ratio of talking to listening, your talk speed, the amount and type of filler words you used, and your "shortest and longest spiel."

Then there's AI-based transcription software like Fathom transcription, which (like Zoom's smart recording feature) records, transcribes, highlights, and summarizes what you're saying in a virtual conversation. I mean, come on: How cool and useful is that?

I have a coaching client who always turns on her Fathom notetaker when we're on Zoom working on developing her keynotes. The session transcriptions—which are clear, detailed, and well-organized—have been a useful reference as we've finessed her talks (and have freed up my client from taking notes so she can be more present with me).

To help you engage with your audiences in real time, there are awesome survey tools. Software like Poll Everywhere, Mentimeter, and MeetingPulse let you poll your audience via their smart phones right in the moment, which can be especially useful with a big audience (or a virtual audience).

I use a QR code provided by Talkadot to get instant audience evaluations of my presentation in exchange for a downloadable gift (like an e-workbook). This app has freed me (and my administrative assistant) from printing and distributing paper evaluations and painstakingly adding individual contact information into my database. Every time I use it, I do a happy dance.

And if you need a little help putting your slide decks together, apps/software like Canva and Prezi offer gorgeous presentation templates that are easy to use and fun to play with.

Virtual Reality: The New Frontier (IR, VR, And AI, Oh! My!)

The fact is, the tech world is brimming with fun and useful apps and high-end tools that, creatively applied, can take your presentations to a whole new level of impact. Incorporating elements of virtual reality (VR) into talks, for example, is a growing trend that I think will become commonplace when the technology becomes more user- (and wallet-) friendly. I've been lucky to be in the audience on two occasions when I've seen it employed to advantage by professional speaker colleagues.

The first time I witnessed VR (brilliantly) in action was when Mike Rayburn, a master-level guitarist, blew the doors off the ballroom at the National Speakers Association's annual convention by performing a harmonized duet of Beethoven's Fifth Symphony with a talking, guitar-playing, three-dimensional hologram of himself.

The second example of a memorable presentation using cutting edge VR technology also occurred at the National Speakers Association's Influence Convention. It was delivered both in the flesh by Sylvie Di Giusto and by various holograms of herself (wearing different outfits!) that popped in and out. If that wasn't remarkable enough, her presentation also utilized projections of three-dimensional, animated visuals (like a school of fish swimming by and around her as she talked) to illustrate her points.

Both presentations necessitated months and months of practice and preparation (presence principle five) because of the timing and complexity of the technology needed to pull them off.

Both presentations were deeply impressive from a visual (and in Mike's case, sonic) standpoint.

And, frankly, both presentations also risked having the audience *ooh* and *aah* over the technology rather than the underlying message the speaker was trying to convey, which can be a drawback of letting flashy technology take center stage. Technology—even technology as simple as a PowerPoint deck, much less a mind-blowing VR-based presentation—can overshadow your humanity and diminish your Charismatic Presence as a speaker if you let it.

That said, all these years later, I'm still talking about those presentations. This speaks to the power of creatively applied, thoughtfully chosen, and extremely well-rehearsed technology components incorporated into presentations by experienced speakers.

Trending: Bite-Sized, Minimal, And Visual

Besides the greater emphasis on incorporating technology in presentations, either from the creation or the delivery standpoint, there is another overall trend I think (and hope) is here to stay: making maximum impact in a minimal amount of time. Less really is more.

Here's what that means:

- Shorter presentations (much to the relief of, well, everyone)

- Bite-sized bits of information that are easy to digest

- Pared-down slide decks with clean, uncluttered visuals (and very little text) that add to (rather than detract from) the message

- One big takeaway point per slide

This preference for minimalistic presentations that are more bite-sized than mega-sized is, I believe, a reflection of our shrinking collective attention span, which, according to a study by Microsoft Corp., has dropped from around twelve seconds to eight seconds (one second less than that of a goldfish, apparently) within the past twenty years.[36] This lowered attention span is no doubt a reflection of the increased need to process the everyday barrage of audio and visual data that is a hallmark of the information age. What this means for you as a speaker is that you've got to catch your audience's attention faster and work harder to keep it once you've got it.

We've also gone gaga for videos and eye-catching images (thank you YouTube, TikTok, Instagram, and smartphone cameras). Audiences, especially younger ones, are accustomed to receiving information through short, punchy videos and images that tell a story quickly and make points sticky. So, if you want to be relevant, hop on the visual bandwagon.

The trend toward short but compelling presentations with uncluttered, eye-catching visuals serves both the audience and the speaker. The simpler, clearer, and more concise your message, the more your audience can ingest it—and the more you can focus on the most important thing of all: genuinely connecting with your audience.

What Will Stay And What Will Go?

Over time, some of the awesome apps and tech I've mentioned might very well become old news, replaced by even cooler technology. I have no doubt that won't be the case with the paradigm-changing technologies like AI content-development tools, virtual meetings, and VR, which are already on their way to becoming an essential part of the fabric of our lives.

As far as some of the presentation development and delivery trends I pointed out—like leaning toward minimalism and visuals, visuals, visuals—well, they might have staying power. I say "might" because trends are by their nature changeable and never-ending, like waves on a beach, so you never know what might be coming next.

What should you do in the face of this avalanche of tools, technology, and ever-changing trends? I suggest you explore them, have fun with them, and learn them well. Do your best to keep up with them, without letting them rule you.

Above all, don't let them prevent you from creating a genuine, human, relatable connection with your audience.

To ensure that your humanity leads out, no matter what technology you choose to use (or don't use) or trend you embrace, honor the evergreen principles I've shared in this book:

- Know thyself

- Be thyself

- Prepare thyself

- Commit thyself

- Turn thyself on (so you can turn other people on)

Because, like AI, and the need to communicate ideas in general, these foundational principles are also here to stay.

When you honor the five presence principles, you fan the flame of your precious, powerful Charismatic Presence. And the message you share becomes even more magnetic to the audiences fortunate enough to hear you speak.

Remember:

You matter.

Your words matter.

Show up, step up, and speak up with your Charismatic Presence on high.

And let your words be heard.

Into The Future

Play With AI. Noodle around and get comfortable with using ChatGPT or another generative AI platform. For example, have it help you position your presentation by asking it to pinpoint the needs and challenges of your specific audience or client; create an outline based on your finished presentation that you can use to rehearse with; or create a summary of your presentation to use when promoting it.

Embrace Visuals. Add more images and bits of video to your presentations to create more engagement and visual variety.

Stay Current, But Find A Balance. On one hand, be conscious of presentation-based trends in AI and tech, and embrace the ones that make your presentation prep or delivery easier and better. On the other hand, don't feel compelled to master every single trend that comes along.

Up The Human Factor. Remember to fold personal stories and humor into your presentations—they are timeless, human, and relatable, and boost your Charismatic Presence.

Appendix

Essential Eleni-isms

A n axiom, as defined by the *Merriam-Webster* dictionary, is "a statement accepted as true,"[37] like "supply equals demand." I like to think of them as little, memorable nuggets of distilled wisdom.

The coaching clients who work with me and the members of my training and keynote audiences have all heard me speak my defining axioms, or what I now call my Eleni-isms. I utter these succinct Eleni-isms regularly, knowing that the more I do so, the more my messages will resonate and stick with the folks I'm speaking to.

I also encourage my coaching clients to winnow down their key points into brief, precise, and catchy phrases. Axioms are memorable and thus repeatable. Every time a member of your audience remembers your axiom, the message you've shared with them is reinforced. And every time they repeat your axiom to someone else, your message is spread to a wider audience.

Words have power; and your willingness and ability to distill your key points into concise, precise axioms adds to that power.

Here are a few Eleni-isms that support the teachings in this book:

- Practice builds confidence, confidence builds presence, and presence is power.

- Presence equals being present.

- Connect first, speak second.

- It's not about being perfect; it's about being human.

- Step into the murky middle of discomfort.

- Turn an icky moment into a sticky moment.

- Turn an "oops!" into an opportunity.

- Strive for excellence, not perfection.

- Overflow with your yumminess.

- Messy is connect-y.

- Fear cannot hit a moving target.

- Action trumps fear.

- Dare to unlock and unleash.

- When you're sphinctered up, you're not breathing. And if you're not breathing, you're not thinking.

- When you shrink to fit, you take a hit.

- Work with a strong intention.

- There's freedom in the form.

- Bring yourself to aliveness.

- Maximize your three presence planes.

- Surrender to the stage.

- Speak in eighth-grade English.

- Lift names, nouns, and numbers up and out on a silver platter.

- Let your words be heard.

- Let your point drop in silence.

- Prime your point with a pause.

- Take your flag and plant it in your point.

- Banish wishy-washy.

- Beige doesn't read from the stage.

- Use your words to change your world.

Example Of A
Speaking Vision Statement

I wrote this in advance of trying out a new keynote presentation in front of an audience for the first time, which is always a little scary.

October 9, 2019

I'm super excited because today's the day I give my new Claim The Stage keynote presentation for the very first time.

I feel ready, because I spent most of the past sixty days finessing and then rehearsing this keynote. The presentation feels totally like me, drenched with my sense of life and sense of humor. I believe in my message with all my heart, and I can't wait to share it with my audience.

I did my vocal exercises in the shower, and a verbal speed-through of the opening and closing of my presentation, and so my voice is warm and ready. Because I took the time to do a thorough job blowing out my hair and applying my makeup, I feel polished and pretty. I put on my favorite black leggings, black boots that make me feel like a superhero, a vibrant, flowing multicolored tunic and sharp-looking, free-flowing jacket that's easy to move and breathe in and do a last-minute mirror check: Yep, I look and feel good.

After a hug and kiss from Jim, I hop into my car, already preloaded with my props, guitar, gear, computer, and books and CDs for my product table. Getting into the habit of using a presentation checklist so I don't forget anything critical and packing up my car the night before a gig, sure has lessened my game-day anxiety.

I get to the venue hotel early enough for a decent sound check with the tech crew in the empty ballroom, making sure that my headset mic and my acoustic guitar have the right volume and tone. Because I take the time to carefully set up the stage as I need it to be, with my portable music stand instead of a lectern, and my acoustic guitar firmly propped on its stand, I feel secure.

I pace the stage to get a sense of its depth and breadth and speak a power phrase or two aloud to the empty room: "I am here," I say, laying claim to the space around me. Then I step off the stage and watch as conference attendees are invited into the room—mostly women and a few men, here for personal and professional development. I make a point to meet and greet a few folks as they settle into their seats, which always energizes me.

Ten minutes before the presentation, I retreat into a quiet corner, where I practice my F.B.I. preshow technique: I ground myself, manage my breathing, and remind myself why I'm here: to encourage the women in the audience to step out of the wings and into the spotlight at work and in the world. Right before I'm introduced, I touch the pearl ring I'm wearing on my right hand and remember the woman who gave it to me: "Ma," I whisper, "I dedicate today's presentation to you. Be with me here today; give me your strength and courage." When my name is called, I step onto the stage, my heart beating a little quickly in my chest, my senses on "go!"

I stand center stage and take a breath in silence, feeling the expectant eyes of the audience. I search for a friendly, smiling person in the first row, and smile back at them, feeling a warm connection. Then I speak the first words of the story that opens my presentation.

From the moment I start, to the moment I finish, I am present, breathing, relaxed. I am conscious of the audience, but in a good way, connecting to them with eyes and heart. I take my time telling my stories, and make sure to clearly articulate my main points and supporting evidence. The audience is so responsive, laughing, listening, sometimes even tearing up.

Sharing my stories and perspective is such a joy! And when I finally pick up my guitar to sing my song, the room is hushed, and I remember how much I love to sing, especially songs I have written that speak my truth.

When I'm done, the audience is on their feet, applauding, and I am over the moon. My host is as thrilled as I am. I plop myself down at my product table and spend half an hour signing books for the audience members who buy them, giving and getting hugs, enjoying brief but meaningful conversations, and fielding inquiries for potential speaking engagements.

In the car on the way home, l look back on the day feeling a great sense of accomplishment and pride. I'm happy that I did what I said I was there to do in relationship to the audience. The keynote flowed and touched hearts and minds as I hoped it would, with only a few areas that need a little tweaking and finessing. I'm now even more excited at the prospect of giving the keynote again and again and again to audiences of women who are gathered in the name of improving themselves and making their difference.

Acknowledgments

This book is informed by my decades of firsthand experience acting, singing, and speaking on countless stages large and small. The fumbles and failures I've experienced in my efforts to maximize my performance ability and my Charismatic Presence have been as valuable to my learning and growth as any of my successes.

All along my journey, I have had top-of-the-line teachers and mentors guiding me and helping me back to my feet when I've stumbled or struggled. This is why, first and foremost, I want to thank the acting teachers and directors who have graced my life with their wisdom and whose techniques I continue to pass along through the clients I coach and train. They include Ora Lichtenstein and Steven Byk from my time at the Walworth Barbour International School in Israel (and Mr. Irving Bloom, my ninth-grade English teacher, who told me I had skills as a writer and "might want to think about using them someday." After three books, countless blog posts, and four CDs of original songs, he just might have been right); Richard Rousseau from Canton High School in Massachusetts; John Emigh, Julie Adams Strandberg, John Wilmeth, and the late, great James O. Barnhill, from my years at Brown University; Michael Howard (a complete and total game-changer) and Warren Robertson in my heady years in New York City; and Brian Reise and Michael Bofshever in Los Angeles.

Directors who inspired and challenged me to take my work to the next level include Anne Bogart ("Could be more!"), Tom O'Horgan, Liviu Ciulei, and Robert Ellenstein.

To these brilliant creatives, who made an indelible mark on my life and work, pushing me kindly but firmly to take more risks and embrace my vulnerability and authenticity, I say: I am who I am, and I do what I do because of you, for which I am forever grateful.

This book was also informed by the thousands of people I have coached or trained over the years, whose courage and commitment to overcoming obstacles as speakers and presenters has continuously expanded my skillsets and knowledge base. Their trust in me has been humbling, and their progress and accomplishments in our work together deeply gratifying. If you are a client, or audience member from a training or speaking engagement, who is reading this, thank you for being open to my teaching and perspective, and for teaching me valuable lessons in return. This book would not have been written without you, and there are not enough pages in it to list you all and adequately sing your praises.

Thanks, also, to the meeting planners—again, too many to mention—who have hired me (sometimes again and again) to share my insights with audiences far and wide. A particular shout-out to Edward Valdez, head of global training at Sartorius, and Laura Denton, director of faculty development at the University of Michigan Medical School, who have brought me in to work with their people for many years. I am grateful for your faith in me, and for your friendship. And Ed, we will always have London and a double grand piano bar as a shared memory.

A blast of gratitude to my mastermind partners (and beloved friends) Karen Jacobsen and Lesley Everett. Thank you for continuously encouraging me to reach my potential in business and in life. Our conversations, retreats, meals, manicures, and shared tears and laughter have buoyed me through some truly trying times.

I would be utterly remiss if I didn't mention the colleagues and pals met and made through the National Speakers Association of Michigan who inspire me to greatness: Dr. Sherene McHenry, Mimi Brown, John B. Molidor, Geri Markel, Greg Peters, Breeda Miller, Marylin Semonick, and Marylin Suttle, I'm talking about you! I have learned so much about what it takes to be a high-level professional speaker through my association with the National Speakers Association—both the national organization and my local (Michigan) chapter. If you want to push yourself toward even greater mastery as a speaker, run, don't walk, to your nearest NSA chapter, or check out nsaspeaker.org.

This book would not have been born without the push, the patience, and the eagle eyes of my publisher, editor, and friend, Henry DeVries, at Indie Books International. You "get" me, Henry, which makes working with you easy, fun, and fruitful. A big thanks to the rest of my team at Indie Books International, including Devin DeVries, Suzanne Hagen, Lisa Lucas, Gail Sevrens, Mike DeTuri, and Melissa Farr (who designed the perfect cover). Without your ministrations, this book would still be floundering in a folder on my computer.

To Marty Somberg of Somberg Design, thank you for the superb Charismatic Presence graphics that accompany the principles I teach in this book. You are a consummate professional and first-class creative, and it's been a total joy to work with you for the last two decades. Also, much gratitude to Maggie Marinaro for designing my adorable Moe and Schmoe illustration, and Leesa Thompson for the gorgeous back cover photo.

And then, of course, there is my mentor, coach, and beloved friend, Mark LeBlanc. Your guidance took my fledgling coaching and training career and ratcheted it to the next level of professionalism and impact. I am immensely grateful for your presence in my life.

My acknowledgements would not be complete without thanking Jim Fleming, the incredible man I'm so lucky to call my husband. You've believed in my dream of creating a coaching, training, and speaking business since the moment I shared the idea with you over two decades ago. Your wisdom and calm spirit have helped me navigate the sometimes turbulent waters of business ownership. You are my rock, no two ways about it, and I love you forever.

Finally, thanks to the Boy Who Ate The World, my late older brother, George Michael Kelakos. George was walloped by COVID-19 in 2020 and died of complications from the disease after more than three years of intense challenge and struggle. He was a world traveler with an international business, a masterful musician, an advanced-degree martial artist, a bon vivant and a warrior on every level. If anybody epitomized the soul stirring, magnetic life force of a Charismatic Presence on max, it was George. I wrote this book in fits and starts throughout the nightmare years of George's dance with COVID. He lived with Jim and me for some of that time, allowing us the grace to tend to him as he fought like hell to heal. There's no question that the content of this book is imbued with George's spirit and that, as one of my biggest champions, he would have been thrilled that I finished it at last.

About The Author

Eleni Kelakos, CSP*, The Speaker Whisperer, is a presence and presentation expert and the president of the Eleni Group, established in 2003. She uses performance techniques learned over twenty years as a professional actor and award-winning, nationally touring singer-songwriter to help business leaders worldwide speak with more authenticity, confidence, and impact.

When she's not coaching individuals or facilitating training at companies like General Motors, Allstate, and Little Caesar's Pizza, Eleni practices what she preaches, firing up hearts and minds with her signature keynote presentations at conferences, summits, and retreats.

The daughter of a career diplomat, who lived in Paris, Rome, and Israel through her mid-teens, Eleni relishes her work with an international clientele hailing from such countries as Belgium, Australia, South Africa, India, Germany, China, the United Kingdom, and the United Arab Emirates.

A double major in theater and semiotics from Brown University, Eleni is a past president of the National Speakers Association of Michigan. She has sung the national anthem at Shea Stadium for three (winning) Mets games and has produced four acclaimed CDs of her original songs. Her book, *Touch the Sky: Find Your Voice, Speak Your Truth, Make Your Mark*, was a gold medal winner of the 2014 Global Ebook Awards. Her second book, released in 2022 through Indie Books International, *Claim the Stage: A Woman's Guide to Speaking Up, Standing Out, and Taking Leadership*, hit number one best-seller status on Amazon.

Eleni is the recipient of an Ignitors Medal from *Creative Washtenaw*, in recognition of "a phenomenal history of leadership to advance the arts, sciences, and humanities."

She lives happily in Ann Arbor, Michigan, with her husband, Jim, and her big, snuggly, red cat, Max.

What is a CSP? Eleni is proud to have been awarded a Certified Speaking Professional designation. The CSP designation, which was established in 1980, is conferred by the National Speakers Association (NSA) to speakers who have met strict qualifying criteria. Fewer than one in five members of the National Speakers Association have been able to meet the CSP's rigorous eligibility requirements. This means that when you hire a CSP, you can be assured that the speaker is a proven professional capable of delivering presentations with the highest level of value and engagement.

To book Eleni as a speaker, or inquire about coaching, write to:
eleni@theelenigroup.com
Or visit www.theelenigroup.com.

Works Referenced And Notes

1   Olivia Fox Cabane, *The Charisma Myth* (BookPress Publishing, 2020),
    5-6

2   *Merriam-Webster.com Dictionary*, s.v. "charisma," accessed September 12,
    2024, https://www.merriam-webster.com/dictionary/charisma.

3   Fox Cabane, *Charisma Myth*, 4

4   Carmine Gallo, "Billionaire Warren Buffett Says This 1 Skill Will Boost
    Your Career Value by 50 Percent," *Inc.*, January 5, 2017, https://www.inc.
    com/carmine-gallo/the-one-skill-warren-buffett-says-will-raise-your-value-
    by-50.html.

5   Nick Morgan, "Why We Fear Public Speaking And How to Overcome
    It," Forbes.com, March 30, 2011, https://www.forbes.com/sites/
    nickmorgan/2011/03/30/why-we-fear-public-speaking-and-how-to-
    overcome-it/

6   Carmine Gallo, "New Survey: 70% Say Presentation Skills Are Critical
    for Success," *Forbes*, September 25, 2014, https://www.forbes.com/sites/
    carminegallo/2014/09/25/new-survey-70-percent-say-presentation-skills-
    critical-for-career-success/?sh=4244eb088890.

7   Elizabeth Barrett Browning, "How Do I Love Thee? (Sonnet 43)," line 1.

8   Catherine Gewertz, "What Do Employers Want in a New Hire? Mostly, Good Speaking Skills," *Education Week*, August 28, 2018, https://www.edweek.org/teaching-learning/what-do-employers-want-in-a-new-hire-mostly-good-speaking-skills/2018/08.

9   "Hi-Diddle-Dee-Dee," lyrics by Ned Washington, *Pinocchio*, directed by Bill Roberts et al. (Walt Disney, 1940).

10 Kyle Buchanan, "Peter Dinklage on 'Cyrano' and Life After 'Game of Thrones,'" *New York Times*, December 22, 2021, https://www.nytimes.com/2021/12/22/movies/peter-dinklage-cyrano.html.

11 Luc Chinman and Jen Juneau, "Julia Louis-Dreyfus Shares Favorite Advice She Has Gotten from Celebrity Women on Her Podcast," *People*, June 29, 2024, https://people.com/julia-louis-dreyfus-shares-favorite-advice-from-celebrity-women-exclusive-8667652.

12 All stories in this book are true, but most of the names have been changed for the sake of privacy.

13 Stephen N. Lambden, "Delphic Maxim 01: 'Know Thyself!'" Hurqalya Publications: Center for Shaykhī and Bābī-Bahā'ī Studies, UC Merced, last revised and expanded October 1, 2016, https://hurqalya.ucmerced.edu/node/297.

14 Eleni Kelakos, *Claim the Stage! A Woman's Guide to Speaking Up, Standing Out, and Taking Leadership* (Indie Books International, 2021), 44-45.

15 Lauren Martin, "Scientists Say It Only Takes 66 Days To Change Your Life, If You're Strong Enough," *Elite Daily*, October 6, 2014, https://www.elitedaily.com/life/motivation/need-stop-bad-habit-need-66-days/784244.

16 Jason Wachob, "Yes, You Can Change Your Brain: How To Do It In 5 Steps, From A Neuroscientist," *Mind Body Green*, July 15, 2020, https://www.mindbodygreen.com/articles/5-steps-to-change-your-brain-from-neuroscientist?srsltid=AfmBOophP8z9yHkSPVYZn6L2O9i5qMyeWVYdh3VAH8bV09m8d3W-CddU.

17 Barbra Streisand, *My Name Is Barbra* (Viking, 2023), chap. 2, Kindle.

18 Streisand, *My Name Is Barbra*, chap. 2.

19 Eleni Kelakos, *Touch the Sky: Find Your Voice, Speak Your Truth, Make Your Mark*, (Eleni Kelakos Enterprises, 2013),107.

20 Kelakos, *Claim the Stage!*, 50.

21 Dr. Seuss, *Happy Birthday to You!* (Random House, 1959).

22 Marguerite Ward, "4 Public Speaking Lessons from the Class that Changed Warren Buffett's Life," *CNBC*, February 3, 2017, https://www.cnbc.com/2017/02/03/4-public-speaking-lessons-that-changed-warren-buffetts-life.html.

23 Alexa Tarantino with Paul Anthony, Grand Hotel, Mackinac Island, Michigan, in-person interview, September 2, 2023.

24 Steve Swavely, *Ignite Your Leadership: The Power of Neuropsychology to Optimize Team Performance* (Indie Books International, 2023).

25 Brian Seibert, "Everybody Dance Now! 'Here Lies Love' Dictates Your Dance Moves," *New York Times*, August 4, 2023, https://www.nytimes.com/2023/08/04/arts/dance/here-lies-love-annie-b-parson-choreography.html.

26 Kim Elsesser, "The Debate on Power Posing Continues: Here's Where We Stand," *Forbes*, October 2, 2020, https://www.forbes.com/sites/kimelsesser/2020/10/02/the-debate-on-power-posing-continues-heres-where-we-stand/.

27 Parasympathetic Nervous System (PSNS), Cleveland Clinic (website), accessed September 25, 2024, https://my.clevelandclinic.org/health/body/23266-parasympathetic-nervous-system-psns.

28 Streisand, *My Name Is Barbra*, chap. 46.

29 Alexa Tarantino with Paul Anthony, Grand Hotel, Mackinac Island, Michigan, in-person interview, September 2, 2023.

30 Tina Fey, "25 Quotes About Improv," Voiceone.com, accessed November 4, 2024, https://www.voiceone.com/verve-posts/25-quotes-about-improv.

31 Gia Kourlas, "Finding Freedom and Feminism in Ballet. (It's Possible.)," *New York Times,* updated April 10, 2023, https://www.nytimes.com/2023/04/05/arts/dance/balanchine-feminism-ballet.html.

32 Mary Lemmer, "How Leadership Can Improve Your Leadership and Life," Ted.com, February 2018, https://www.ted.com/talks/mary_lemmer_how_improv_can_improve_your_leadership_and_life?utm_campaign=tedspread&utm_medium=referral&utm_source=tedcomshar.

33 Alexa Tarantino with Paul Anthony, Grand Hotel, Mackinac Island, Michigan, in-person interview, September 2, 2023.

34 Salam Slim Saad, "The Seven-Second Rule: What Is It, And How Does It Affect You," Wideimpact.com, accessed October 2024, https://wide-impact.com/blog/the-7-second-rule-what-is-it-and-how-does-it-affect-you/.

35 "What Are the Best Ways to Use Technology to Improve Your Public Speaking Feedback and Evaluation?" LinkedIn, accessed September 26, 2024, https://www.linkedin.com/advice/0/what-best-ways-use-technology-improve-your-public-rzxwf.

36 Jamie DuCharme, "You Now Have A Shorter Attention Span Than A Goldfish," Time.com, May 14, 2015, https://time.com/3858309/attention-spans-goldfish/.

37 *Merriam-Webster.com Dictionary*, s.v. "axiom," accessed September 25, 2024, https://www.merriam-webster.com/dictionary/axiom.